First World War
and Army of Occupation
War Diary
France, Belgium and Germany

32 DIVISION
Divisional Troops
219 Machine Gun Company
16 March 1917 - 28 February 1918

WO95/2385/6

The Naval & Military Press Ltd
www.nmarchive.com
Published in association with The National Archives

Published by

The Naval & Military Press Ltd

Unit 10 Ridgewood Industrial Park,

Uckfield, East Sussex,

TN22 5QE England

Tel: +44 (0) 1825 749494

www.naval-military-press.com

www.nmarchive.com

This diary has been reprinted in facsimile from the original. Any imperfections are inevitably reproduced and the quality may fall short of modern type and cartographic standards.

© Crown Copyright
Images reproduced by permission of The National Archives, London, England, 2015.

Contents

Document type	Place/Title	Date From	Date To
Heading	WO95/2385 32 Division 219 Coy Machine Gun Corps March 1917-Feb 1918		
Heading	32nd Division Divl Troops 219th Coy. Machine Gun Corps 1917 Mar-1918 Feb.		
Heading	219 Company Machine Gun Corps. Attached 32nd Division. War Diary For The Month Of March 1917 To Dec 1918. Vol I.		
War Diary		16/03/1917	31/03/1917
Heading	War Diary Of 219th Machine Gun Coy. From April 1st 1917 To April 30th 1917 Volume 2		
War Diary	Douilly	01/04/1917	01/04/1917
War Diary	Ch De Pommery	02/04/1917	02/04/1917
War Diary	Savy	03/04/1917	15/04/1917
War Diary	Auroir	16/04/1917	18/04/1917
War Diary	Foreste	19/04/1917	21/04/1917
War Diary	Languevoisin	22/04/1917	30/04/1917
Operation(al) Order(s)	Coy Operation Orders No. 2. Appendice No. 1	21/04/1917	21/04/1917
Miscellaneous	Training Programme-219 M.G. Coy Appendice No 2	28/04/1917	28/04/1917
Miscellaneous	Training Programme No. 2. Appendice No. 3	05/05/1917	05/05/1917
Heading	War Diary Of 219th Machine Gun Coy From May 1st 1917 To May 31st 1917 Volume 3		
War Diary	Languevoisin	01/05/1917	14/05/1917
War Diary	Curchy	15/05/1917	15/05/1917
War Diary	Rosieres	16/05/1917	16/05/1917
War Diary	Thennes	17/05/1917	29/05/1917
War Diary	Villers Bretonneux	30/05/1917	31/05/1917
Miscellaneous	Training Programme No. 2. Appendice No. 1	05/05/1917	05/05/1917
Miscellaneous	Training Programme No. 3. Appendice No. 2	12/05/1917	12/05/1917
Operation(al) Order(s)	Operation Order No. 4. Appendice No. 3	14/05/1917	14/05/1917
Operation(al) Order(s)	Operation Order No. 5. Appendice No. 4	15/05/1917	15/05/1917
Operation(al) Order(s)	Operation Order No. 6. Appendice No. 5		
Miscellaneous	Training Programme No. 5. Appendice No 6	26/05/1916	26/05/1916
Operation(al) Order(s)	Operation Order No. 7. Appendice 7	29/05/1917	29/05/1917
Heading	War Diary Of 219th Machine Gun Coy From June 1st 1917 To June 30th 1917 Volume 4		
War Diary	Villers-Bretonneux	01/06/1917	01/06/1917
War Diary	Neuf-Berquin	02/06/1917	14/06/1917
War Diary	Godwaerswelde	15/06/1917	16/06/1917
War Diary	Teteghem	17/06/1917	17/06/1917
War Diary	St. Ideswald	18/06/1917	19/06/1917
War Diary	Nieuport	20/06/1917	29/06/1917
War Diary	Coxyde	30/06/1917	30/06/1917
Operation(al) Order(s)	Operation Order No. 8. Appendice No. 1	01/06/1917	01/06/1917
Operation(al) Order(s)	Operation Order No. 9. Appendice No. 2	02/06/1917	02/06/1917
Operation(al) Order(s)	Operation Order No. 10. Appendice No. 3	10/06/1917	10/06/1917
Operation(al) Order(s)	Operation Order No. 11. Appendice No. 4	13/06/1917	13/06/1917
Miscellaneous			
Operation(al) Order(s)	Operation Order No. 12. Appendice No. 5	14/06/1917	14/06/1917
Operation(al) Order(s)	Operation Order No. 13. Appendice No. 6	15/06/1917	15/06/1917
Operation(al) Order(s)	Operation Order No. 14. Appendice No. 7	19/06/1917	19/06/1917

Type	Description	Start	End
Operation(al) Order(s)	Operation Order No. 15. Appendice No. 8	29/06/1917	29/06/1917
War Diary	Coxyde	01/07/1917	11/07/1917
War Diary	Nieuport	11/07/1917	20/07/1917
War Diary	Bray Dunes	21/07/1917	26/07/1917
War Diary	Coxyde	27/07/1917	31/07/1917
Operation(al) Order(s)	Operation Order No. 16. Appendix No. 1	30/06/1917	30/06/1917
Operation(al) Order(s)	Operation Order No. 17. Appendix No. 2	06/07/1917	06/07/1917
Operation(al) Order(s)	Operation Order No. 18. Appdx No. 3	17/07/1917	17/07/1917
Operation(al) Order(s)	Operation Order No. 19. Appdx No. 4	18/07/1917	18/07/1917
Miscellaneous	Training Programme For We July 28th 1917. Appdx No. 5		
Operation(al) Order(s)	Operation Order No. 20. Appdx No. 6	26/07/1917	26/07/1917
Operation(al) Order(s)	Operation Order No. 21. Appdx. 7	31/07/1917	31/07/1917
Operation(al) Order(s)	Operation Order No. 22. Appdx 8	31/07/1917	31/07/1917
Heading	War Diary. of 219th Machine Gun Coy From August 1st 1917 To August 31st 1917 Volume 6		
War Diary	Nieuport	01/08/1917	11/08/1917
War Diary	Coxyde	12/08/1917	14/08/1917
War Diary	Bray Dunes	15/08/1917	26/08/1917
War Diary	Coxyde	27/08/1917	31/08/1917
Operation(al) Order(s)	Operation Order No. 23. Appendix No. 1	10/08/1917	10/08/1917
Operation(al) Order(s)	Operation Order No. 24. Appendix No. 2	14/08/1917	14/08/1917
Miscellaneous	Training Programme. Appendix No. 3		
Miscellaneous	219 MG Coy Training Programme For Week Ending August 25th 1917. Appendix No. 4	25/08/1917	25/08/1917
Operation(al) Order(s)	Operation Order No. 25. Appendix No. 5	28/08/1917	28/08/1917
Operation(al) Order(s)	Operation Order No. 26. Appendix No. 6	28/08/1917	28/08/1917
Operation(al) Order(s)	Operation Order No. 27. Appendix No. 7	28/08/1917	28/08/1917
Heading	War Diary of 219 Machine Gun Coy. From September 1st 1917. To September 31st 1917. Volume 7		
War Diary	Nieuport	01/09/1917	30/09/1917
Operation(al) Order(s)	Operation Order No. 28. Appendix No. 1	02/09/1917	02/09/1917
Operation(al) Order(s)	Operation Order No. 29. Appendix No. 2	02/09/1917	02/09/1917
Operation(al) Order(s)	Operation Order No. 30. Appendix No. 3	14/09/1917	14/09/1917
Operation(al) Order(s)	Operation Order No. 31. Appendix No. 4	16/09/1917	16/09/1917
Operation(al) Order(s)	Operation Order No. 32. Appendix 5		
Operation(al) Order(s)	Operation Order No. 33. Appendix No. 6	23/09/1917	23/09/1917
Operation(al) Order(s)	Operation Order No. 34. Appendix No. 7	26/09/1917	26/09/1917
Operation(al) Order(s)	Operation Order No. 35. Appendix No. 8		
Operation(al) Order(s)	Operation Order No. 36. Appendix No. 9	29/09/1917	29/09/1917
Heading	War Diary. Of 219 Machine Gun Coy From October 1st 1917 To October 31st 1917 Volume 8		
War Diary	Nieuport	01/10/1917	06/10/1917
War Diary	Bray Dunes	07/10/1917	24/10/1917
War Diary	Teteghem	25/10/1917	25/10/1917
War Diary	L'Erkels Brugge Area	26/10/1917	31/10/1917
Operation(al) Order(s)	Operation Order No. 37. Appendix 1	02/10/1917	02/10/1917
Operation(al) Order(s)	Operation Order No. 38. Appendix 2	05/10/1917	05/10/1917
Operation(al) Order(s)	Operation Order No. 39. Appendix 3	05/10/1917	05/10/1917
Operation(al) Order(s)	Operation Order No. 40. Appendix 4	06/10/1917	06/10/1917
Miscellaneous	Training Programme. 219th. Machine Gun Company Week Ending October 13th 1917. Appendix 5	13/10/1917	13/10/1917
Miscellaneous	Training Programme. 219th. Machine Gun Company Week Ending October 20th 1917. Appendix 6	20/10/1917	20/10/1917
Miscellaneous	Training Programme. 219th. Machine Gun Company Week Ending October 27th 1917. Appendix 7	27/10/1917	27/10/1917

Operation(al) Order(s)	Operation Order No. 41. Appendix 8	24/10/1917	24/10/1917
Operation(al) Order(s)	Addendum No 1 To O.O. No. 41. March Discipline. Appendix 8		
Miscellaneous	Breakdown		
Operation(al) Order(s)	Operation Order No. 42. Appendix 9	25/10/1917	25/10/1917
Miscellaneous	Training Programme 219th Machine Gun Company Week Ending November 3rd 1917. Appendix 10	03/11/1917	03/11/1917
Heading	War Diary Of 219 Machine Gun Coy. From Nov. 1st 1917. To Nov. 30th 1917. Volume 9		
War Diary	L'Erkels Brugge	01/11/1917	10/11/1917
War Diary	Arneke	11/11/1917	11/11/1917
War Diary	Winnezeele	12/11/1917	12/11/1917
War Diary	Popperinghe	13/11/1917	21/11/1917
War Diary	Irish Farm	22/11/1917	24/11/1917
War Diary	Canal Bank	25/11/1917	30/11/1917
Miscellaneous	Training Programme 219 Machine Gun Company. Week Ending November 3rd 1917. Appendix No. 1	03/11/1917	03/11/1917
Miscellaneous	Training Programme 219 Machine Gun Company Week Ending November 10th 1917. Appendix No. 2	10/11/1917	10/11/1917
Operation(al) Order(s)	Operation Order No. 43. Appendix No. 3		
Operation(al) Order(s)	Operation Order No. 44. Appendix No. 4		
Operation(al) Order(s)	Operation Order No. 45. Appendix No. 5		
Miscellaneous	Training Programme 219th Machine Gun Company Week Ending November 24th. 1917. Appendix No. 6	24/11/1917	24/11/1917
Operation(al) Order(s)	Operation Order No. 46. Appendix No. 7	21/11/1917	21/11/1917
Operation(al) Order(s)	Operation Order No. 47. Appendix No. 8		
Heading	War Diary Of 219 Machine Gun Coy. From December 1st 1917. To December 31st 1917. Volume 10		
War Diary	Ypres Canal Bank	01/12/1917	02/12/1917
War Diary	Ypres	02/12/1917	31/12/1917
Operation(al) Order(s)	Operation Order No. 48. Appendix No 1	29/11/1917	29/11/1917
Miscellaneous			
Miscellaneous	Acknowledge		
Operation(al) Order(s)	Addendum No. 1 to O.O. No. 48	30/11/1917	30/11/1917
Miscellaneous	Appendix "A" Machine Guns.		
Miscellaneous	Fire Organisation Orders. L. Battery	29/11/1917	29/11/1917
Miscellaneous	Fire Organisation Orders. K. Battery.	29/11/1917	29/11/1917
Operation(al) Order(s)	Operation Order No. 49. Appendix No 2	27/12/1917	27/12/1917
Operation(al) Order(s)	Operation Order No. 51. Appendix No 3	29/12/1917	29/12/1917
War Diary	Peselhoek	02/09/1917	02/09/1917
War Diary	Ghyvelde	04/09/1917	07/09/1917
War Diary	Oost Dunkerke	08/09/1917	30/09/1917
Miscellaneous	32nd Division.	31/10/1917	31/10/1917
War Diary	Oost Dunkerke	01/10/1917	07/10/1917
War Diary	Coudekerque	21/10/1917	23/10/1917
War Diary	Coudekerque	20/10/1917	20/10/1917
War Diary	St Jean	01/11/1917	18/11/1917
Heading	War Diary Of 219th Coy. Machine Gun Corps. From January 1st 1918 To January 31st 1918 Volume 11		
War Diary	Canal Bank	01/01/1918	03/01/1918
War Diary	Grasse Payelle	04/01/1918	20/01/1918
War Diary	Langemark Area	21/01/1918	25/01/1918
War Diary	Elverdinghe Area	26/01/1918	31/01/1918
Operation(al) Order(s)	Amendment No. 2 to Operation Order No. 50. Appendix No. 1	31/12/1917	31/12/1917
Operation(al) Order(s)	Addendum No. 1 to Operation Order No. 50	30/12/1917	30/12/1917

Type	Description	Date From	Date To
Operation(al) Order(s)	Operation Order No. 50	29/12/1917	29/12/1917
Miscellaneous	Appendix A. Transport March Discipline.		
Operation(al) Order(s)	Amendment No. 2 to Operation Order No. 52		
Operation(al) Order(s)	Amendment No. II To Operation Order No. 52		
Miscellaneous	To O.C. 219 M.G. Coy.	01/02/1918	01/02/1918
Operation(al) Order(s)	Operation Order No. 52	30/12/1917	30/12/1917
Miscellaneous	Training Programme. 219 Machine Gun Company Week Ending January 12th 1918. Appendix No. 2	12/01/1918	12/01/1918
Miscellaneous	Training Programme. 219 Machine Gun Company Week Ending January 19th 1918. Appendix No. 3	19/01/1918	19/01/1918
Miscellaneous	Training Programme. N.C.Os. 219 Machine Gun Company Week Ending January 19th 1918	19/01/1918	19/01/1918
Miscellaneous	Training Programme. Attached Men. 219 Machine Gun Company Week Ending January 19th 1918	19/01/1918	19/01/1918
Operation(al) Order(s)	Operation Order No. 53. Appendix No. 4	17/01/1918	17/01/1918
Miscellaneous	Appendix A. Transport March Discipline.		
Operation(al) Order(s)	Operation Order No. 54	15/01/1918	15/01/1918
Operation(al) Order(s)	Operation Order No. 55. Appendix No. 5	25/01/1918	25/01/1918
Operation(al) Order(s)	Operation Order No. 56. Appendix No. 6	27/01/1918	27/01/1918
Miscellaneous	Training Programme. 219 Machine Gun Company. Week Ending January 26th 1918	26/01/1918	26/01/1918
Miscellaneous	10. Command.		
Heading	War Diary Of 219th. Machine Gun Company. From February 1st. 1918 To February 28th. 1918 Volume 12		
War Diary	Elverdinghe Area	01/02/1918	10/02/1918
War Diary	Woesten Area	11/02/1918	12/02/1918
War Diary	Boesinghe Area	13/02/1918	28/02/1918
Operation(al) Order(s)	Operation Order No. 57. Appendix "A".	11/02/1918	11/02/1918
Operation(al) Order(s)	Operation Order No. 58 Appendix "B".	15/02/1918	15/02/1918
Operation(al) Order(s)	Operation Order No. 59. Appendix "C".	25/02/1918	25/02/1918
Operation(al) Order(s)	Operation Order No. 60. Appendix "D".	27/02/1918	27/02/1918

WO95/2385
32 DIVISION
219 COY MACHINE GUN CORPS

MARCH 1917 – FEB 1918

32ND DIVISION
DIVL TROOPS

219TH COY. MACHINE GUN CORPS

~~MAR 1917 DEC 1918~~

1917 MAR — 1918 FEB

Original.

Vol I

219 Company. Machine Gun Corps.
attached 32ⁿᵈ Division.

War Diary.

for the month of

March 1917.
to
Dec 1918

In the Field.
1ˢᵗ. 4 - 17.

Army Form C. 2118.

fol. 1.

WAR DIARY
INTELLIGENCE SUMMARY.
(Erase heading not required.)

Instructions regarding War Diaries and Intelligence Summaries are contained in F. S. Regs., Part II. and the Staff Manual respectively. Title pages will be prepared in manuscript.

Place	Date	Hour	Summary of Events and Information	Remarks and references to Appendices
	16/3/17	6 pm	Embarked at Southampton (on Queen Alexandra Manchester Importer)	
		11 pm	Disembarked at Havre. Strength 9 officers 146 other ranks 7 horses 47 mules 16 guns. Deficiencies 1 officer 31 other ranks.	
	17/3/17		}	
	18/3/17		}	
	19/3/17		} No 2 Rest Camp Havre	
	20/3/17		}	
	21/3/17		}	
	22/3/17		}	
	23/3/17		Journeyed by train from Havre to La Flaque arriving 8 pm	
	24/3/17		Left La Flaque 9 am and marched to Humcourt arrived there 3 pm and billeted	

Army Form C. 2118.

WAR DIARY
INTELLIGENCE SUMMARY.
(Erase heading not required.)

Place	Date	Hour	Summary of Events and Information	Remarks and references to Appendices
	26/3/17		Left Avremcourt 9 am and marched to Hesse arrived there 3pm and billeted -	
	27/3/17		In billets at Hesse awaiting orders	
	28/3/17			
	29/3/17		Left 8 am (Hesse) and marched to Bancourt. No 2 & 4 Section entered the line with 97" and 14" Brigades respectively. Remainder in rest billets at Bancourt	
	30/3/17		No 2 and 4 Sections in the line with 97" and 14" Brigades respectively. Remainder in rest billets at Bancourt	
	31/3/17		Sections 2 and 4 in the line as above. Remainder in rest billets at Bancourt. 6.30 pm H.Q. and reserves moved forward to Doilly.	

R C [signature] O.C. 219 COY
MACHINE GUN CORPS

CONFIDENTIAL.

Vol 2

WAR DIARY

OF

219th MACHINE GUN COY.

(From April 1st 1917 — 15th April 30th 1917)

(VOLUME 2)

WAR DIARY

INTELLIGENCE SUMMARY

Army Form C. 2118.

Place	Date	Hour	Summary of Events and Information	Remarks and references to Appendices
DOUILLY	1st April	9.30 a.m	H.Qrs marched at 9.30am and arrived at GERMAINE at 11 am. The Company attached to 14th Brigade for attack on ETREILLERS and BOIS DE SAVY. Advanced through ROUPY and occupied positions North of the village to provide covering fire for infantry advance. Heavily shelted whilst advancing to positions - two men wounded. Infantry attack successful.	MHA REF. 62c S.E. $\frac{1}{20000}$
		5.30 p.m	Ordered to concentrate Company at Ch. de POMMERY and established H.Qrs there at 7.45 p.m.	HQJ
CH. DE POMMERY	2nd	4. am	No. 2 and 3 Sections reported at Ch. de POMMERY at 4 am and were sent to ETREILLERS and advanced in moved through hollow on right of BOIS DE HOLNON Pushed on to left flank of HOLNON to provide covering fire for infantry who captured all objectives and six field guns.	HQJ
		1 P.m.	Sections withdrawn to Ch. de POMMERY.	
SAVY	3rd		No. 2 and 4 Sections 2/Lt EDWARDS and ALLEN - pushed up to support 2nd MANCHESTERS. No. 1 and 3 in reserve at SAVY FRANCILLY SELENCY.	HQJ
SAVY	4th		Heavy fall of snow interfered with operations. Dispositions unchanged.	HQJ
SAVY	5th		14th Brigade is bereleived and Company attached to 97th Brigade for attack on FAYET This attack to be made when French have advanced on St. QUENTIN No. 2 and 4 Sections in line in front of SELENCY and FRANCILLY SELENCY. No. 3 section in reserve	HQJ
SAVY	6th		Situation unchanged dispositions unchanged	HQJ
SAVY	7th		Situation unchanged dispositions unchanged	HQJ

Army Form C. 2118.

WAR DIARY
or
INTELLIGENCE SUMMARY

(Erase heading not required.)

Instructions regarding War Diaries and Intelligence Summaries are contained in F. S. Regs., Part II. and the Staff Manual respectively. Title pages will be prepared in manuscript.

Place	Date	Hour	Summary of Events and Information	Remarks and references to Appendices
SAVY	8th April		Situation unaltered normal. Lt. R.C. STONE, Second in Command, killed by shell whilst walking through HOLNON. Draft of 30 received to form No 1 Section and complete Company strength.	H.C.H
SAVY	9th		No 4 Section – 2/Lt. EDWARDS - relieved by No 1 Section under 2/Lt. BEARD in FRANCILLY SELENCY. No 4 Section returned to billets in SAVY. Lt. DAWSON of 96th M G Coy assumed temporary Command, Lt. F.A. HOOPER from 106th M G Coy posted as Second in Command Authority.	H.C.H
SAVY	10th		Dispositions unaltered.	H.C.H
SAVY	11th		Dispositions unaltered.	H.C.H
SAVY	12th		Dispositions unaltered. 2/Lt ROWNTREE casualty from shell shock and rheumatism replaced by 2/Lt E.G. LORD from rest billets.	H.C.H
SAVY	13th	9.a.m	Attack on FAYET to be made at 4.30 a.m on the 14th Company to co-operate with 97th M.G. Coy as laid down in their O.O. No 17 and Agenda thereto.	H.C.H
		8.15 p.m	Nos. 3 and 4 Sections in reserve moved into the line and took up positions in vicinity of Copse M33 Central where they were joined by half of No 1 Section. Lt. H.G. HARCOURT from 184 M G Coy appointed to Command 2ig Company.	H.C.H
SAVY	14th	4.30 a.m	Nos 3, 4 and No 1 Subsection opened indirect fire on following Sensitive points Enemy trench running N's through M34 b 9.0. to M34 b 9.9. N.O.N. MIN. MINNECHET and cross roads M34 6.5.5. to S 6.6.2.3. Village of FAYET. Road from M36 C.5.5. to S 6.b.2.3. Suspected battery position M35 d 1.2. / 20 contour in M29c.	Ref. Sheet 62 B S W Edition 2
		5.30 a.m	Indirect fire ceased. No 4 Section – 2/Lt EDWARDS dug themselves in and laid their guns to protect left flank of FAYET. 2/Lt POTTER - No 3 Section sent out scouts to ascertain if he could advance to M34 b 6.5. but found this was still held by the enemy but it was cleared at 4 p.m. and he then advanced there to support A Coy of the KOYLI. and No 1 subsection.	H.C.H

Army Form C. 2118.

WAR DIARY
INTELLIGENCE SUMMARY.
(Erase heading not required.)

Place	Date	Hour	Summary of Events and Information	Remarks and references to Appendices
SAVY	14th	5.30 a.m.	The remaining Sub-section of No1 under 2/Lt BEARD pushed forward to approx S10 d 5.2 and then to M36 c 6.2 to support C Coy 16 HLI.	HGS
		12 noon	No2 Section under 2/Lt E.G. LORD advanced to approx M36.d 5.4 to support C Coy KOYLI. One gun team under Sgt McRAE lost touch but eventually reported to No1 Subsection 2/Lt BEARD and remained there until the end of the action. One gun of No2 Section arrived just in time to help the KOYLI drive back a counter attack. The enemy were just advancing over the ridge when the gun opened fire and drove them back. Sergt McEWEN and Pte MILAN in particular behaved exceedingly well. CASUALTIES 2 killed 6 wounded, one gun knocked out.	HGS
SAVY	15th	9am	Dispositions unchanged. Heavy shelling on advance	HGS
		3 pm	No1 Sub-section - 2/Lt BEARD - relieved by Sub-section No1 under 2/Lt EDWARDS	HGS
SAVY	16th	9 am	Dispositions unchanged	HGS
		6 pm	Company withdrawn from line and marched to billets at AUROIR	HGS
AUROIR	16th	11 pm	Arrived in Billets at AUROIR. Company comfortably settled. 2/Lt A.N. PEACHEY reported for duty	HGS
"	"	1 pm	Commenced reorganisation of Company and equipment.	HGS
"	17th	9 am	Billets AUROIR - reorganisation continued	HGS
"	18th	9 pm	Removed to billets at FORESTE. Company comfortably settled by 2 pm	HGS Ref Sheet 62B S.W. Edition 2
FORESTE	19th 20th		Reorganisation of Company and equipment	HGS

Army Form C. 2118.

WAR DIARY
or
INTELLIGENCE SUMMARY.

(Erase heading not required.)

Instructions regarding War Diaries and Intelligence Summaries are contained in F.S. Regs., Part II. and the Staff Manual respectively. Title pages will be prepared in manuscript.

Place	Date	Hour	Summary of Events and Information	Remarks and references to Appendices
FORESTE	21st April		Reorganisation and preparations for move.	Appendix C.O. No 1 H.C.H
LANGUEVOIS-IN	22nd	9 am	Marched to LANGUEVOISIN. Arrived 1.5 p.m. Company settled in good billets	H.C.H
do.	23rd to 28th		Training as per training programme No 1.	Appendice No 2
do.	29th		Church parades and recreational training	
do.	30th		Training as per training programme No 2	Appendice No 3

H.C. Harcourt Lt.
O.C. 219. COY. M G CORPS

APPENDICE No 1
COY No 3

COY OPERATION ORDERS. No 2
21.4.17

REF. MAP.
sheet 66.P.
1-40,000.

1) **MOVE.** The Coy will march to LANGUEVOISIN tomorrow 22nd.
2) **ROUTE** DOUILLY - MATIGNY - VOYENNES - NESLE.
3) **STARTING POINT.** The head of the column will pass starting point E.15.C.7-8. at 9.am.
4) **PARADE.** Coy will parade at 8.50 am.
5) **DRESS.** Full marching order - less overcoats.
6) **ORDER OF MARCH.** HQ - Nos 1 2 3 4 Sections Transport.
7) **INSPECTION.** Section Officers will inspect their Sect before marching on to the market.
   All billets and ground around to be left scrupulously clean, and refuse pits to be filled in.
8) **OVERCOATS.** will be carried on limbers rolled in bundles by gun teams. All limbers to be packed ready for march by 8 am.
   Officers Valises to be at Coy Stores by 7-45 am.
9) **ONE G S WAGON** from D.A.C. will report to Coy Stores at 8 am. It will be packed immediately and will form the end of the column as it passes.
10) **MARCH DISCIPLINE.** Strict march discipline is to be maintained. Section Officers will warn all NCOs to this effect.
11) **FALLING OUT.** All other ranks must be informed that any man falling out will be called upon to give an explanation as to the cause. CASES OF MEN FALLING OUT "SHOULD NOT OCCUR.
12) **MARKERS.** One marker from H Qtrs and one per section will report to CSM at 8-45 am on parade ground.

Issued at 6.30 pm

COPY No 1 HQ.
     " 2 HQ
     — 3 War Diary.
     " 4 32 Div HQ G.
     " 5 " " " Q.
     " 6 2/LT EDWARDS
     " 7 " POTTER
     " 8 " LORD
     " 9 " ALLIN
     " 10 " HYDE
     " 11 " CSM
     " 12 " CQMS
     " 13 " Spare

H.C. Harcourt Lieut,
O.C. 219. COY. M G CORPS

APPENDICE No 2

Training Programme – 219 M.G. Coy   April 28th 1917

Week Ending April 28th 1917

	9–10	10–11	11.15–12.30	2–3	LOCATION	REMARKS
23rd	Yrs of Eqpt Gen Insp.	Mechanism	Stripping and cleaning	Anti Aircraft sights + firing	Behind No 4 Billet	As depot will be reduced to 1 Off & 2 per Company, any beginners men who require special training
24th		Mechanism	I.A. Gun Drill Belt Repairs	Squad Drill with arms	Languevoisin T.27.C	I A must be given thorough attention
25th	Action	I.A. Prolonged Stoppages	I.A. Stripping Repairs	Lecture on A.A. Sights by 2/Lt Allin	Central Sheet 66D	Sections will fit A.A. sights during last morning parade
26th	Comb.d Drill by Sections	Principles of the Ground & Direction of the Direction	Action from Limber	Lecture on I.F. by S. Offs		The training of N.C.O's and the choice of positions will receive special attention
27th	I.F.	Comb.d Drill	Action from Limber	Section Drill		
28th	Adv.d G.Drill	I.A.	Section in open warfare	Lecture to N.C.O. No 15 on Map Reading		Remainder of Section Depot Strength under Sgt. McLaren

Strict discipline & paying of compliments is to be insisted on throughout the training. Sections will be thoroughly inspected on first parade and a high standard of cleanliness maintained.

After 3 pm Recreational training will be carried out commencing with Inter Section Competitions.

Note issued to Section Officers are to be kept in mind.

O.C. 219 COY. M.G. CORPS

APPENDIX N° 3
5th May 1914

219 Machine Gun Company
Week Ending

Training Programme N° 2

	8:30 9:0	9-10	10-11	11:15-11:45	11:45-12:30	2-3	Remarks
Apl 30 Monday		Action	S.A.	Visual Training	J.R.	Points to B.A.	Sections half hour revolver drill after 2:30 pm
May 1 Tuesday	N°1+2 Section		Fire Direction	Range Firing			Application of Strict attention to be paid to correct range
	N°3+4 Section	Action with light tripod	S.A.		J.R.	Turning wide still for movement	Use of cover "Camouflage"
May 2 Wednesday	N°3+4 Section		Fire Direction	Range Firing			
	N°1+2 Section	Action with light tripod	S.A.		J.R.	Turning wide still for movement	Use of cover & camouflage
May 3 Thursday		Overhead fire & Bombard Drill	S.B.J. Sighting	Sections in attack (Yo-work as a Company)		Overhead Fire and Limber Stores	The ciphid holding & sight setting & maintaining sight (extra time on range if required)
May 4 Friday		In direct fire	Trench Drill	J.A.		2-3:30 Sections in Attack	
May 5 Saturday		Sections at Section Officers disposal; work to be handed to O.R. by 6pm		J.A.			

PHYSICAL TRAINING

Range finding Class will be at work throughout the week under Sgt. Macrae.
Hours of work 9-11 a.m. as otherwise arranged to suit weather conditions.
Scouts will be trained daily under 2nd Lieut.

29-4-17
[signature]
2nd Lieut. O.C. 219 Coy. M.G. Corps

ORIGINAL.

Confidential.

Vol 3

War Diary.

of

219th. Machine Gun Coy.

Volume. 3.

From May. 1st 1917.   To. May 31st 1917.

Army Form C. 2118.

WAR DIARY
INTELLIGENCE SUMMARY.
(Erase heading not required.)

Instructions regarding War Diaries and Intelligence Summaries are contained in F. S. Regs., Part II. and the Staff Manual respectively. Title pages will be prepared in manuscript.

Place	Date	Hour	Summary of Events and Information	Remarks and references to Appendices
LANGOEVOISIN	May 4th & May 5th		Training as Programme No 2. Capt. A Leeson assumed command of Company vice Lt. H G Harcourt.	Appendice No 1
	May 3rd May 6th		Church Parade and recreational training	Nil Nil Nil
do	May 7th & 12th		Training as Programme No 3	Appendice No 2
do	13th		Church parade and recreational training	Nil
do	14th	9 a.m. 2 p.m.	Tactical scheme in conjunction with 97th Infy. Bde. Preparations for move.	Nil
CURCHY	15th		March from Languevoisin to Curchy. Company comfortably settled in billets at 10 a.m. Remainder of day spent in cleaning and preparation for further move. See operation order No 4	Appendice No 3
ROSIERES	16th	12 noon	March from Curchy to Rosieres. Company settled in billets at Rosieres. See operation order No 5.	Appendice No 4 Nil
THENNES	17th	12 noon	March from Rosieres to Thennes. Company settled in billets at Thennes. See operation order No 6	Appendice No 5 Nil

Army Form C. 2118.

WAR DIARY
INTELLIGENCE SUMMARY.
(Erase heading not required.)

Instructions regarding War Diaries and Intelligence Summaries are contained in F. S. Regs., Part II. and the Staff Manual respectively. Title pages will be prepared in manuscript.

Place	Date	Hour	Summary of Events and Information	Remarks and references to Appendices
THENNES	18th	9 am	Overhauling guns, spare parts and filling ammunition belts.	Nil
do	19th	2 pm	Improvements to billets.	
do	19th	9.30 am	Lectures and demonstrations of "creeping barrage fire" by Section Officers.	Nil
do	20th		Church Parade and recreational training	Nil
do	21st to 26th		Training as Training Programme No. 5. Throughout the week special attention was given to instruction in "barrage fire" and M.M. The use of direction and elevating dials; N.C.Os were given training in the use of map and compass for indirect and barrage fire.	Appendice No 6
do	27th		Church Parade.	Nil
do	28th	9 am 11.30 am	Further training in use of direction and elevating dials, and M. Immediate action	Nil
do	29th	9 am	Practice in use of belt filling machine, packing limbers and Gal preparing for move.	

(A7692). Wt W12839/M1293. 75,000. 1/17. D. D. & L., Ltd. Forms/C.2118/14.

Army Form C. 2118.

WAR DIARY
or
INTELLIGENCE SUMMARY.
(Erase heading not required.)

Instructions regarding War Diaries and Intelligence Summaries are contained in F. S. Regs., Part II. and the Staff Manual respectively. Title pages will be prepared in manuscript.

Place	Date	Hour	Summary of Events and Information	Remarks and references to Appendices
VILLERS BRETONNEUX	30th	7am	March to VILLERS BRETONNEUX. Company arrived in billets 9.30am. Remainder of day spent cleaning up and improving billets.	O.O.N°9 Appendix N°9.
do	31st	9am	Training in use of Anti-aircraft machine guns.	do.

signed
CAPT.
COMDG. 219 COMPANY M.G. CORPS.

Appendice No 1
5th May 1914

2.19 M.G. Company
Week Ending

Training Programme No 2.

	9-10	10-11	11.15-11.45	11.45-12.30	2-3	Remarks
Apl 30 Mond	Action	J.A.	Visual Training	J.O.	Bomb & B.A.	Section half trained yesterday drill afts 2.30 pm
May 1 Tues	No 1 & 2 Sect	Ind Section Rightly tripod	Range firing	J.O.	Dummy Mts for mind & assembly	Application stopping strict attention to be
May 2 Wed	No 3 & 4 Sect	Ind Section Left w tripod	Range firing	J.O.	Dummy Mts for mind & assembly	paid to correct rapid discipline holding &
May 4 Mon	No 1 & 2 Section	Range firing Left Tripod	Range firing	J.O.	Mt sof corrects camouflage	sighting & extra time in every
May 5 Thurs	Ind head fire & combine a Drill fighting	Section sight testing	Sections in attack (to work ios a Company)	Dismantle of 13.05 Limbs Stores	required
May 4 Fri	Indirect fire	Trench Drill	J.A.	Stopping & Repair	2. 3.30 Sections in attack
May 5 Sat	Section at action officers disposed & employed with to be handed to O.R. by 6 pm				dispersal disposed to O.R. by 6 pm	

Range firing Class will be at work throughout the week under Sgt MacRae. Hours of work 9-11 or as otherwise arranged to suit weather conditions. Scouts will be trained daily under Lt Lord.

29-4-17

Appendice No 2.

12th May 1914

219 M.G. Coy.
Week Ending
Training Programme No. 3.

Hours	9-10	10-11	11-15 - 11-45	11-45 - 12-30	2 - 3.30	5 - 6 pm	Remarks
May 7th Monday	Gun Drill in Box Respirators	Duties as Orderlies	Loading and unloading pack mules		Musketry Instruction	5-6 pm Nt. 6 O/s Msh. Headquarters S.O.	
8th Tuesday	Nos 1 & 2 Gun Drill Sections	Range Practice (Stoppages) Limber Drill			Loading - unloading pack mules		The range practice to be field (at any box formation) 25 yds Ring, grouping application
9th Wednesday	No. 3 & 4 Gun Drill Sections	No.3 & 4 Gun Drill in Box Respirators	Range Practices (Stoppages) Limber Drill	Duties as Orderlies	Musketry		The range practice to be first practice box grouping 25 yards Range young - grouping + application
10th Thursday	Nos 1 & 2 Gun Drill in Box Respirators		Route March.	Duties as Orderlies	Musketry		
11th Friday	Practical Exercise		Field Work		Lecture by S.O. m indirect fire		
12th Saturday		Tactical Exercise			Lectures by loading + unloading Pack mules	5-6 pm Nt 6 O/s Msh Headquarters O.S.	

In the Field
5-5-14

219 M G C°Y   MAY 14TH 1917.

Appendix No 3

OPERATION ORDER No. 4.

Map Reference Sheet 66.D. 1:40000.

MOVE. The 219th M G Coy (less 1 subsection) will move from LANGUEVOISIN to CURCHY on the morning of the 15th inst.

ORDER OF MARCH. Headqtrs. Sections No's 1. 2. 3 and 4. Transport.

DRESS. Full marching order less overcoats.

TRANSPORT will form up on the road, the head of the Transport to be opposite the main entrance to the Transport Lines, not later than 6-10 a.m.

PARADE. The Coy will parade in line on the Parade Ground at 5.45 a.m. and will move off from Languevoisin at 6.20 am.

MARCH DISCIPLINE. The strictest march discipline will be observed during the march. There are to be no blank files, and nobody is allowed to fall out on the line of march without written permission from the OC C°Y.

BILLETS Section Officers will report "Billets clean" to OC C°Y not later than 6. am.

LATRINES Latrines will be closed by squad detailed by C S Major not later than 5.30 am.

BILLETING PARTIES. Lt J W Beard will report to Staff Captain at the Church CURCHY at 6-30 am to arrange billets.

BLANKETS. All blankets to be on Limbers by 5:30 am.

REVEILLE 4 am.
BREAKFAST 4.30 am

Issued at 7.45 pm.

       Ian A Leeson
       O C mdg 219 M G Coy. Capt.

Copy No 1   No 1 Section Officer.
" " 2   2 " "
" " 3   3 " "
" " 4   4 " "
" " 5   TRANSPORT OFF
" " 6   FILE.
" " 7   WAR DIARY.
" " 8
" " 9
" " 10

Appendice No 4.

219. M.G.Coy   May 15" 1917.

OPERATION ORDER No 5.

Reference Maps. Sheets 66^D and 66^E 1-40,000.

MOVE. The 219" MG Coy, less one subsection, will move from CURCHY to ROSIERES on the morning of the 16 inst.

ROUTE. HALLU - CHILLY - MAUCOURT - MAHARICOURT - ROSIERES.

ORDER of MARCH. Hdqtrs - No 1 section with section transport followed by Nos 2, 3, and 4 sections in similar formation, followed by HQ limber - Water Cart and Mess Cart.
The Guard will march with Hdqtrs.

DRESS. Full marching order.

PARADE. The Coy will parade under section arrangements to be on the road adjoining Transport, and facing N.W. at 4 am. - To halt in front of section limbers.

TRANSPORT will be on the same road at section intervals at 4 am.

MARCH DISCIPLINE. Attention is again called to the necessity of enforcing MARCH DISCIPLINE. No man is allowed to fall out on the line of march without a chit signed by the OC Coy. Any man disregarding this order is liable to Court Martial.

BILLETS Section Officers are responsible that billets are left clean and latrines closed.

BLANKETS All blankets to be on limbers by 2.30 am.

BILLETING PARTIES. Lt J.W.P. Beard will report to the Staff Captain at the Church Rosieres, at 6 am accompanied by two signallers, all to be on bicycles.

RATIONS. Rations issued tonight are tomorrows rations and the unconsumed portion must be carried by the men themselves.

Reveille 2-15 am
Breakfast 2-45 am

Issued at 6.15 pm.

               CAPT.
COMDG. 219 COMPANY M.G. CORPS.

Copy No 1   No 1 S Off
"   2   2 "
"   3   3 "
"   4   4 "
"   5   T Off.
"   6   FILE
"   7   War Diary.
"   8
"   9
"   10

Appendice No 6.

OPERATION ORDER No 6.

REF MAPS. HMIENS 1/100,000.

MOVE. The 219 M.G. Coy less 1 subsection will move from ROSIERES to THENNES on the morning of 17th -

ROUTE. CAIX - IGNACOURT - HUBERCOURT - DENUIM Cross-roads at point 104 -

ORDER OF MARCH Same as Operation Order No 5.

DRESS. Full marching order. Nobody is allowed to march without packs except brakesmen and Transport. In the event of wet weather tomorrow, at the start greatcoats will not be worn but water proof sheets will be slung over the shoulders.

PARADE The Coy will parade under Section arrangements on the road in the billeting area facing SW at 4.30.am. The head of the column to be outside Hdqtrs billet and halt in front of Section limbers -

TRANSPORT. will be on the same road at section intervals at 4.30 am.

MARCH DISCIPLINE. One case occurred today of a man falling out without permission - Section Officers must instruct their sections as to the punishment liable to men disregarding the order and falling out without O.C. Coy chit.

BILLETS Despite orders billets in some cases were left dirty this morning. Section Sergts must be present to supervise their respective billets -

BLANKETS All blankets to be on limbers by 3.am -

BILLETING PARTIES. Lt J W Page - Beard and two Signallers will report to Staff Captain at the Church, HANGUARD at 5.15 am.

Reveille 2.45 am
Breakfast 3.15 am
Issued at 9-10 pm.

Capt
Comdg 219 MG Coy -

Copy No 1   No 1 S. Off
     2   2 " "
     3   3 " "
     4   4 " "
     5   T.O.
     6   FILE.
     7   WAR DIARY
     ?   "   "

Appendice No 6

219 M.G. Coy.
Week ending 27th May 1917

Training Programme No 5

Date	6.15-7.45	9-9.30	9.45-12.30	2-5
21 Monday	Square Drill with Arms	P.T.	Barrage fire	The men having failed to fully explain to section before any possible demonstration is given
22 Tuesday	Square Drill with Arms	P.T.	9.45-12 Barrage fire	2-5.30 Lecture by O.C. Coy Overhead
23 Wednesday	Square Drill with Arms	P.T.	9-12.30 Barrage fire	Special attention to be paid to instruction of Overhead Dial workings thereon
24 Thursday	Square Drill with Arms	P.T.	9am-12.30 Route March & Inspection of 66 Coy	
25 Friday	Square Drill with Arms	P.T.	Barrage fire	Special practice in creeping barrage
26 Saturday	Square Drill with Arms	P.T.	9.45-10.30 Squad drill with Arms	10.30-1230 Barrage fire	10.30-1230 Special actual instruction in firing of creeping barrage in

J. Woodward
CAPT.
COMDG. 219 COMPANY M.G. CORPS.

219 M.G.Coy.   Appendice No 7.   May 29. 1917

OPERATION ORDER No. 7.

Map Reference sheet 62D 1/40,000.

MOVE. The 219 M.G.Coy will move from TAENNES to VILLERS - BRETTONEAUX on the morning of the 30th inst.

ORDER OF MARCH. HQrs — No 1 section with section Transport followed by Nos 2, 3 & 4 sections in similar formation. HQ limber. Water cart and mess-cart. The Guard will march with HQ".

DRESS. Full marching order.

PARADE. The Coy will parade under section arrangements to be on the main MOREUIL - AMIENS road facing NW at 7 am. Head of column to be about 300 yds NW of main billet. Transport will be on the same road at section intervals at 7 am.

MARCH DISCIPLINE. March discipline must be strictly maintained. No man is allowed to fall out on the line of march without a chit signed by the OC Coy. Any man disregarding this order is liable to Court martial.
Brakesmen must not hang on to the limbers and nothing whatsoever is to be carried on the water cart.

OFFICERS CHARGERS to be fully equipped and to carry feeds, water buckets, head ropes, picketing ropes and spare shoes. Only regulation bridles to be worn.

BILLETS. Section Officers are responsible for leaving billets in a clean condition and will report to the OC Coy by 6.45 am. Officers are individually responsible that their own billets are left clean. The CSM will see that the latrines are closed by 6.15 am.

BLANKETS all blankets to be on the limbers by 5.15 am.

BILLETING PARTIES. Lt Ju Page Beard will report to Staff Capt at Church Villers Brettoneaux at 6.30 am accompanied by two signallers, all to be on bicycles.

RATIONS. The unconsumed portion of the days rations will be carried by the men.

Reveille. 5 am
Breakfast 5.30 am.
Issued at 3-15 pm

_____ CAPT.
COMDG. 219 COMPANY M.G. CORPS.

Copy No 1 No 1 Section Off
     2   2   "   "
     3   3   "   "
     4   4   "   "
     5   Transport Off
     6   File
     7   War Diary
     8   "   "
     9   Spare
    10   Spare.

Original.

Confidential.

Vol 4

War Diary
of
219th Machine Gun Coy

From June 1st 1917   To June 30th 1917

Volume 4.

Army Form C. 2118.

WAR DIARY

INTELLIGENCE SUMMARY

(Erase heading not required.)

Instructions regarding War Diaries and Intelligence Summaries are contained in F. S. Regs., Part II. and the Staff Manual respectively. Title pages will be prepared in manuscript.

Place	Date	Hour	Summary of Events and Information	Remarks and references to Appendices
VILLERS-BRETONNEUX	1st June		Preparations for move and entraining to new area as per O.O. No 8 *pub*	Appendix No 1
NEUF-BERQUIN	2nd		Detraining at Steenbecque and march to NEUF-BERQUIN. Company settled in good billets at 5.30 p.m.	
do	2nd		Four Sections took over the Anti-aircraft defence of dumps as follows:— No 1 Section at Trent Depot Ref. Sheet 28 S 29 b. "2 Section at Duke of York siding " 28 S 15 b "3 Section at Duke of Connaught siding " 28 T 26 c "4 Section at LaCreche Depot " 36 A Band	See O.O. No 9 *pub* Appendix No 2
			H.Qrs remained at NEUF BERQUIN.	
do	4th 5th 6th 7th		Anti-aircraft duty as above	*pub*
do	8th		At about 10 am ammunition train at Duke of York Siding caught fire and the ammunition commenced exploding. No 17139 L/c POLLARD was with his gun team near the train ran forward and uncoupled the burning trucks from the undamaged ones and with the assistance

WAR DIARY

INTELLIGENCE SUMMARY

Army Form C. 2118.

Place	Date	Hour	Summary of Events and Information	Remarks and references to Appendices
NEUF-BERQUIN	9th		of some men of a Labour Battalion succeeded in saving six loaded trucks. For this deed he was awarded the Military Medal on 16 inst.	
do	10th		Anti-aircraft duty as above.	Appendice No. 3.
do	11th		Sections relieved by ANZAC Troops as per O.O. No. 10	
do	12th 13th		Cleaning up and preparations for move. A competition was held for the smartest turned out section and also the smartest Section Transport. Major Stanley of 97th M.G. Coy acted as Judge and awarded the prizes to No. 3 Section for men and equipment, and to No. 1 Section for Transport.	
do	14th		Move to EECKE Area. See operation order No. 11. Company settled in billets at GODWAESVELDE at 2.30pm	Appendice No. 4.
GODWAES-VELDE	15th		Day Transport resting. Transport Section moved to COUDEKERQUE area as per operation order No. 12.	Appendice No. 5.

Army Form C. 2118.

WAR DIARY
or
INTELLIGENCE SUMMARY.

(Erase heading not required.)

Place	Date	Hour	Summary of Events and Information	Remarks and references to Appendices
GODWAES-VELDE	16th		Company less Transport moved by bus to Coudekerque area and arrived in billets at TETEGHEN at 8 p.m and there joined transport section. See operation order No.13.	Appendice No 6
TETEGHEN	17th	4.30 am	Transport Section left by road for COXYDE area.	Map Reference
		6.30 am	Company less Transport marched to DUNKERQUE and proceeded by barge to FURNES, and marched from thence to ST IDESWALD arriving in billets at 5.30 p.m. The transport Section thereof joined the Company.	Dunkerque 1st Belgium 1:40,000
ST. IDESWALD	18th		Resting.	
do	19th		The Company relieved the French machine guns in the J and Z sub-sectors of NIEUPORT as per operation order No 14	Appendice No 7
NIEUPORT	20th		Relief completed by 2. am Heavy shelling immediately after relief completed	

WAR DIARY

INTELLIGENCE SUMMARY.

Army Form C. 2118.

Place	Date	Hour	Summary of Events and Information	Remarks and references to Appendices
NIEUPORT	20th		Trench warfare. Indirect fire carried out on sensitive points and villages behind the German line. 16000 rounds fired.	JW
do	21st	4 pm	Trench warfare. 9/U Power, Sgt. Green and No 11534 4/Cpl Dowse wounded by whizz bangs whilst reconnoitring positions for emplacements.	JW
		11 pm 6 am	Indirect fire again carried out on villages &c. 16000 rounds fired. Retaliation from enemy with shells and m.g. fire.	
do	22nd		Trench warfare. Impossible to do any work by day as enemy observation is very good and any signs of activity provokes shelling. Indirect fire carried out at night (16000 rounds) and emplacements improved and strengthened.	JW
do	23rd		Ditto. No 67369 Pte. McNulty, J. wounded by shell fire near church in Nieuport. Indirect fire from 11pm to 3am. Enemy retaliating and sweeping our trenches and roads with machine guns. Still very active with artillery.	JW

Army Form C. 2118.

WAR DIARY
INTELLIGENCE SUMMARY

(Erase heading not required.)

Instructions regarding War Diaries and Intelligence Summaries are contained in F. S. Regs., Part II. and the Staff Manual respectively. Title pages will be prepared in manuscript.

Place	Date	Hour	Summary of Events and Information	Remarks and references to Appendices
NIEUPORT	24th		Trench warfare. Enemy still very active with artillery fire, emplacement destroyed at M.30.c.95.45. No casualties. Indirect fire - 16000 rounds carried out on sensitive points. Enemy retaliation with m.g. fire	tuk
"	25th		Trench warfare. Indirect fire - 16000 rounds - from 11pm - 3am. Major W.A. Stanley of 97th M.G. Coy. having been appointed Divisional Machine Gun Officer assumed command of 219th Company, Capt. J. A. Leeson replacing him in command of 97th Coy.	tuk
"	26th 27th 28th		Trench warfare. 16000 rounds indirect fired nightly.	tuk
"	29th		Company relieved by 14th M.G. Coy. (See Operation Order No 15) Relief carried out without a hitch. Enemy very quiet and no shelling.	Appendix No 8. tuk
COXYDE	30th	1.45 am	Arrived JEANNIOT CAMP complete. Billets very comfortable	tuk
		9 am	Day spent cleaning up and reorganising equipment.	tuk

J.W. Meagher Capt.
OOMDG. 219 COMPANY M.G. CORPS

219 M.G.Coy Appendice No 1 June 1st 17

Operation Order No 8.

Map Ref - Sheet No 17. Amiens 1/100.000

MOVE. The 219 M.G.Coy will move from Villers Bretonneux to new area on June 1st. They will entrain at 21-30m on Train No 16.

PARADE. Transport will parade in sufficient time to be at the station not later than 18h 30m. Limbers will be packed complete by 16h. The boy less transport will parade by sections at 19hrs, form up in line opposite the Chateau at the N end of the Rue de la Mairie ready to march off at 20hr.

DRESS. Full marching order - all waterbottles to be filled.

DRESS Officers. Officers must carry both box respirators and smoke helmets.

TRANSPORT Water cart to be loaded full. Horses will be watered as late as possible before entraining. Watering facilities exist in the neighbourhood of the entraining station. These must be reconnoitred and made use of. Nose bags will be carried full and hay nets, and horses will be watered and fed whenever opportunity occurs on journey. Breast ropes, chains & water buckets will be taken. At least 2 men will travel in each horse truck. The Transport Officer of each Unit will entrain his own horses. Grooms & Drivers will act as entraining party.

ENTRAINING Absolute silence to be maintained during entraining. A Senior N.C.O. to be in charge of each conveyance. No men to leave conveyance until the whole unit is entrained, and then only with permission of OC Train. Officers should make themselves acquainted with F S.R. pt 1 para 34-40. Section Officers are reminded that only by strict discipline and attention to detail can efficiency in entraining be obtained. The time taken by each Unit will be recorded.

DETRAINING The same discipline and silence must be observed as in entraining. No man must leave the train until the order is given.

MARCH DISCIPLINE. As roads in new area are narrow and there is a considerable amount of transport road discipline must be strictly maintained all transport especially odd mess. carts must keep strictly to the right.

BILLETS Section Officers are responsible for leaving Billets in a thoroughly clean condition and will report this complete to OC at 19h 30m. Officers are individually responsible for leaving their own billets clean.

RATIONS The rations for the 2nd instant will be carried by the men. The rations for the 3rd to be carried on the supply wagon.

LIGHTING. On arrival in new area every precaution is to be taken to ensure screening of lights directly it is dark, and any offenders will be severely punished.

Issued at 11-40 a.m.

Copies 1/4 S.O.
5 File
6/7 War Diary.

CAPT.
COMDG. 219 COMPANY

OPERATION ORDER No 9. Appendice No 2

Map Refs – sheet 36 ed 6 1/40000; sheet 28 ed.3 1/40000. June 2/17
Hazebrouck 5a ed 2. 1/100,000.

GENERAL. On the 3rd inst four sections of 219 MG Coy will take over the Anti Aircraft Defence of ammunition depots under the II Anzac Corps as follows –

I. No 3 Section under Lt J W Page Beard at Duke of Connaught Siding. Map Ref. sheet 28 T 26 c.

II. No 4 Section under 2Lt J.F. Allin. at LA CRECHE. Depot. ref sheet 36 A 6 b and d.

III. No 2 Section under Lt S L Vincent at Duke of York siding. ref sheet 28. S 15 b.

IV. No 1 Section under 2Lt E G Lord at TRENT Depot – Ref sheet 28 S 27 b.

If the 14th MG Coy took over these positions on the 2nd inst they will be relieved by the above sections, but if the 14th MG Coy did not relieve, Section Officers must report as follows not later than 4 pm –
Ordnance Officer I/c Duke of Connaught Siding in case of (I)
Ordnance Officer I/c Duke of York Siding in case of (III) and IV
In case of II detachment will relieve similar detachment of II Anzac Corp Cyclist Batt.

PARADES. All sections will parade complete with transport opposite their billets facing NW under section arrangements ready to march off from NEUF BERQUIN – at 9.30 am.

ROUTE. (Ref sheet Hazebrouck 5a)
No 2 Section via Vieux Berquin and BAILLEUL.
No 1 Section via RUE PROVOST – DOULIEU – LA VERRIER to cross roads approximately 1 mile W of STEENWERCK – thence North to TRENT Depot.
No 3 & 4 Sections via Rue Provost – Doulieu – La Verrier. Steenwerck and Steenwerck station. thence NW to positions.

RATIONS. All sections will carry rations for 3rd & 4th inst after which they will be rationed by Administrative Commandant 2nd Army Rail head – Feeds and Fodder for horses and mules will be carried for 3rd & 4th inst –

DRESS Full Marching order –

WAGGONS All waggons will be cleaned under section arrangements before marching off –

ANTI AIRCRAFT FITTINGS Each Section Off is responsible for taking one complete set of AA fittings. Further sets will be forwarded on receipt of same.

RELIEF COMPLETE. Section Off must inform OC Coy by word by wire WHISKEY when relief is completed. Officers must not leave their positions on any account without permission of OC Coy –

Coy HQRTS Until accommodation is provided elsewhere Coy HQ will be at NEUF BERQUIN –

Guard. The Guard will join their sections in time to march off with them –

Reveille 6.30 am
Breakfast 7.45 am
Issued at 10.30 p.m.

CAPT.
COMDG. 219 COMPANY M.G. CORPS.

AFTER ORDER.

Route. The route for No 2 Section will be as for No 1 Section as far as TRENT Depot and then via BAILLEUL to destination.

Rations. Rations for the 4th will be drawn by all sections at cross roads ½ mile NE of Le KIRLEM and ½ mile W of STEENWERCK at 11.30am.

Copy Nos 1/4 Sec Off.
5 File
6/7 War Diary
8/9 Spare.

Appendice N°3.
June 10/17.

219 M G Coy

Operation Order 10

Map Ref Hazebrouck 5a ed 2 1/100,000.

Relief. Sections of 219 M.G.Coy at present on AA Duty with I Anzac Corp will be relieved by 2nd Anzac mtd troops. The relief to be completed by 10 a.m. 11"- On completion of relief sections will march to CHQ at NEUF BERQUIN.-

Tents. Tents will be handed over to relieving troops & receipts obtained.

Anti Aircraft Appliances. To be handed over with the exception of those belonging to the Coy. and receipts obtained. Each section should bring back 2 A.A. sights & 1 Drum with fittings complete. and No 4 section will bring the 2 poles belonging to the Coy -

Rations The days rations in hand and the unconsumed portion of the rations for the 11" will be carried by sections. Also fodder for animals.

Dress Full marching order.

Waggons. Section Off will see that all waggons are properly cleaned before moving off

Issued at 2.15 pm

_____ CAPT.
COMDG. 219 COMPANY M.G. CORPS.

Appendice N° 4

219 MG Coy **June 13th/17**

OPERATION ORDER N° 11

Map Ref. Sheet 5a Hazebrouck.

MOVE. The 219 MG Coy will move from NEUF BERQUIN to EECKE area on the morning of the 14th inst. with Section transport.

ORDER OF MARCH. HQrs – N° 1 section followed by N° 2, 3 & 4 sections in similar formation. HQ limber – Water Cart & Mess Cart and GS Wagon. The guard will march with HQ.

DRESS. Full marching order.

PARADE The Coy will parade under Section arrangements to be on the main NEUF BERQUIN – VIEUX BERQUIN road facing north at 7-10 am. Head of column to be opposite N°1 section Billet. Transport will be on the same road at section intervals at 7.10 am.

MARCH Discipline. March Discipline must be strictly maintained. No man is allowed to fall out on the line of march without a chit signed by OC Coy. Any man disregarding this order is liable to a Court Martial. Brakesmen must not hang on to the Limbers and nothing whatsoever is to be carried on the water cart.

OFFICERS CHARGERS. To be fully equipped and to carry feeds, water buckets, head ropes, picketing ropes and spare shoes. Only regulation bridles to be worn.

BILLETS Section Officers are responsible for leaving billets in a clean condition and will report this to OC Coy by 6.45 am. Officers are individually responsible that their own billets

2/

are kept clean. The COs will see that all latrines are closed by 6-15 am

LIMBERS Limbers to be packed by 7-30 am 13th inst. with the exception of the cooking appliances which will be on the limbers not later than 6.15 am

RATIONS The unconsumed portion of the days rations will be carried on the men and rations for the 15th carried on the GS wagon.

Reveille 5 am
Breakfast 5·30 am

[signature] _____ CAPT.
COMDG. 219 COMPANY M.G. CORPS.

Issued at 11-45 am

Copy No	
1	Sect Off No 1.
2	" " 2
3	" " 3
4	" " 4
5	Transpt Off
6	File
7	War Diary
8	-
9	Spare
10	-

Guard.   A guard of 1 NCO and 3 men to be mounted
             over any Lewis armaments they want.

Vehicles.   All vehicles to be thoroughly cleaned under
             Section arrangements not later than
             9 am on the 25 inst.

Dixies   2 Dixies per section to be returned, all
             other material and all offspare Kits &
             men kits must be sent to ordnance with the Lewis...

Issued at 4.45 pm.

Copies 1 — E   2/Lt FE Hyde
        2 —   Lt McManus
        3 —   F.H.
        4 —   War Diary.
        5 —
        6   Spare.

                                    [signature] CAPT.
                            COMDG. 2ND COMPANY M.G. CORPS.

Appendice No 5
June 14 1917

219 MG Coy.

OPERATION ORDER No 12

Map Ref 2h.◦E 27 2◦◦◦◦ 1/40,000

Move — The transport section of 219 M.G.Coy. under 2Lt. Hazenworth Hyde will move from ECKE. on the morning of June 15 and march to Glenworth and reach Q.16.3.8 at 11.34 am. They will form up there and move in other groups of the column with transport units forming up on the road facing N.W. The transport units will situate nearby to ammunition dumps.

PARADE — At 10.15 am ammunition transport [illegible] ... in 3 sections for N.O.C. ... the Coy ... [illegible] transport will form to the E.S.E. of the Road at this point ... is meet at Calar ration ... [illegible] ... is the meet ... be taken.

RATIONS — Rations for 16 meals.

BILLETS — Bn. Route. The Battn. will cover out the march of civilian centres - or under orders of O.C. & Col. 3rd Division.

219 MG Coy   Copy 3   June 15' 1917
         Appendice No 6

Operation Order No 13

Map Ref Sheet Hazebrouck 5ª 1/40000
              Dunkerque 1ª 1/100.000

Move   The 219 MG Coy less transport and personnel detached in O Order No 12 will move from GODEWAESVELDE to COUDEKERQUE on the morning of 16" inst and on arrival come under the orders of GOC 14" Infy Bde.

Order of March   HQrs. No 1 Section followed by No 2. 3 & 4 sections

Dress   Full Marching Order.

Parade   The Coy will parade outside HQ Billet at 4.15 am and march to the embussing point and be embussed in busses marked L not later than 5.45 am.

Discipline.   Strict discipline and quietness must be maintained during embussing, men will be detailed to their various busses before moving off. No man is allowed to enter or leave a bus without permission from the NCO in charge.

Billets   Section Officers are responsible that Billets are left in a sound & clean condition and must report this to OC Coy by 3.45 am

2.

Officers are personally responsible that their own billets are left clean.

RATIONS The unconsumed portion of the Days rations will be carried by the men and three discs per section will also be carried. Water Bottles must be filled.

Reveille 2.45 am
Breakfast 3.15 am.

Issued at 1.0 pm

_____ CAPT.
COMDG. 219 COMPANY M.G. CORPS.

Copy No. 1   Sec Off.
     "   2   CSM
     "   3   War Diary
     "   4   War Diary

Appendice No 7

JUNE 19th 1917

219 MG COY

OPERATION ORDER No 14.

Map Ref sheet Dunkerque 1 & 1/40,000.

Relief The 219' MG Coy will relieve the French M Guns in the D and E Sub-sectors of NIEUPORT. on the nights of 19"/20" June. Sections 1 and 2 in D sub-sector

ORDER of BATTLE No"3 & 4 sections in E sub. sector.

PARADE The Coy will parade at Jonnerel at 5pm. One limber per section and HQ limber only will parade.

ROUTE Conyde – Oost Dunkerke – Nieuport. Coy will not leave Oost Dunkerque before 7:30 pm and will then move at 300 metres interval.

ORDER of MARCH Sections will move in the following order:– No"s 3, 2, 1, HQ.

DRESS Fighting Order.

GUIDES One guide per section at 9 pm to guide Limbers to Nieuport. Loading Point. One guide per sub section will be at Loading point at 10.15 pm to guide teams to gun positions.

RATIONS. Rations for 30° and to draw to be carried by sections on the limbers.

RELIEF. The relief are to report when completed —
                1 "BRANDY": completed by section to commencement
COY Hd Qtrs   when section to be sent to COY HQ by runner.
Gas..   All SOS applications will be taken over originally by section holding taken
               originally frontage.

EXPOSURE. All work to be carried on at night, exposure to aeroplanes during the day, and the fact that any movement in progress has been observed by aeroplane is to be reported immediately to the Coy Commander.

TRANSPORT. On completion of further movement return to Document.

Issued at 11.45 am

ACKNOWLEDGE.

Copy N° 1 ... N° 1 Sec Off
        2 ... " 2 "
        3 ... " 3 "
        4 ... Trans pt Off
        5 ... 14 Inf Bde
        6 ... 14 M.G. Coy.
        7 ... War Diary
        8 ...
        9 ... File
        10 ... File
        11

[signature] CAPT.
COMDG. 219 COMPANY M.G. CORPS.

OPERATION ORDER 15

Map: BELGIUM. DUNKERQUE 1a 1/100000

APPENDICE No 8

29/6/17

RELIEF. The 219th Machine Gun Company will be relieved in the D and E Sub Sections of NIEUPORT by the 14th Machine Gun Company on the night of 29/30th June at 9 pm.

GUIDES Each section will arrange to have one guide per Gun team at the ration dump below the MAISON BLANC at 8.45 pm. Guides from HQ to ration dump will be provided by HQRS

HANDING OVER
All S.A.A and TRENCH STORES will be handed over to incoming company but Section officers are responsible for all Gun equipment, Belt boxes, spare parts, A.A. Appliances, and such company property as dixies and cooking utensils must be brought from the trenches. The position of emplacement, alternative emplacements, lines of fire, fire schemes, work in progress and all possible information in regard to the line are handed over to incoming officers.

TRANSPORT.
H.Q. limber will be at C.HQ at 7 pm. and one complete battle limber per section will be at the ration dump at 9 pm. The transport officer will see that all drivers are acquainted with road to rest camp.

MARCH BACK.
On completion of relief, section officers will see their battle limbers are packed and then move by sections independently to JEANNIOT CAMP. They will see that intervals not less than 100 yards are maintained between sections

COMPLETION.
Completion of relief will be reported to C.HQ NIEUPORT by each section on their way back. If the main NIEUPORT- OOST DUNKERQUE ROAD is being shelled the ZOUAVE ROAD will be used, and a guide will be provided for leading section.

BILLETS. The allotment of billets are as follows.
- HUT. J.2 Officers
- " J.5 No 1 Section
- " J.8 " 2 "
- " J.9 " 3 "
- " J.28 " 4 "
- " J.29 HQRS.

ISSUED AT
PLEASE ACKNOWLEDGE

Hooper
CAPT
COMDG. 219 COMPANY M.G. CORPS

Army Form C. 2118.

WAR DIARY
INTELLIGENCE SUMMARY.
(Erase heading not required.)

219 M.G. Coy Vol 6

Place	Date	Hour	Summary of Events and Information	Remarks and references to Appendices
COXYDE	1st July		Two Sections (No 3 and 4) relieved two sections 96th M.G. Coy in NIEUPORT Sector as per O.O. No 16. Relief completed by 10 p.m. No unusual shelling. Remainder of Coy and Hqrs at COXYDE	Appendix No 1. JHH
"	2nd		Two sections in line fired indirect on enemy strong points in conjunction with artillery "retaliation scheme" 4000 rounds fired. Sections in rest JHH training for "BARRAGE FIRE" and emplacement building	JHH
"	3rd to 5th		Dispositions as on the 2nd Guns in line fired daily in conjunction with artillery and at hostile aircraft	JHH
"	6th		Hostile artillery active and left gun positions suffered one emplacement being blown in and one man (Pte Ashby) wounded	JHH
"	7th		Inter Company relief No.s 1 and 2 Sections relieving No.s 4 and 3 Sections respectively. Relief completed by 10 p.m. No unusual shelling. O.O. No 17 JHH	Appendix No 2.
"	8th		Hostile artillery active two dugouts blown in and No 61654 L/Cpl Owen R No 66869 Pte Edwards G.J and No 17139 4/c. Pollard W.R (M.M) killed. The gun at M28 a.4.5.7 was completely destroyed.	Sheet 12-SW Edition 1a. JHH
"	9th 10th		Dispositions unchanged but enemy artillery still active.	JHH
"	11th		Enemy bombarded all day long with 5.9's and naval guns and attacked our lines in the evening penetrating the 1st and 2nd lines on the left of 1 st Divisional sector The Division on the left were pushed back over the Canal.	

Army Form C. 2118.

WAR DIARY

INTELLIGENCE SUMMARY

(Erase heading not required.)

Place	Date	Hour	Summary of Events and Information	Remarks and references to Appendices
NIEUPORT	11th	4 pm	Gun positions suffered and the left two guns at about M.21.b.4.7.8 were buried but were subsequently recovered	Sheet 11 Sur Edition 1a.
		9 pm	The half Company in reserve were warned to stand to at 10 a.m. and at 9 p.m. received orders to proceed to NIEUPORT and place themselves at the disposal of G.O.C 97th Infty Bgde. who ordered four guns to reinforce the guns at M.21.b.4. 5-9 and the remaining four guns to take up	
do	12th	2 am	Positions in the Redan (M.28.a.b.) These guns got in to position by 7 a.m. In spite of the barrage and the enemies continued use of gas shells. The casualties in the line were few and all remained at duty except Lt J.W Page Beard who fell and broke a knee cap whilst entering NIEUPORT and had to be sent down the line. Capt J.O Cook reported as O.C on the 11th and accompanied the half Company in to NIEUPORT.	duty
		9 am	Shelling much quieter and day spent salvaging as much buried material as possible and reorganizing positions.	duty
do	13th		Situation calm except for artillery bombardment during early hours of morning.	duty
		9.30 pm	Enemy commenced heavy bombardment with gas shells and made NIEUPORT very unhealthy. No casualties resulted to 219 In Coy.	duty
	14th/15th		Day quiet in comparison with preceeding days. During the night the Infantry endeavored to regain the position of trenches lost on the 11th. and the guns of the Company cooperated	duty

Army Form C. 2118.

WAR DIARY
INTELLIGENCE SUMMARY.
(Erase heading not required.)

Instructions regarding War Diaries and Intelligence Summaries are contained in F.S. Regs., Part II. and the Staff Manual respectively. Title pages will be prepared in manuscript.

Place	Date	Hour	Summary of Events and Information	Remarks and references to Appendices
NIEUPORT	15th		With the artillery and barraged sensitive points in the enemy line, firing 62,000 rounds in all. The infantry only met with partial success and were not able to recover all the lost ground. During the night a dugout at approx M 21 d 4.5 was blown in and two men who were sleeping in it killed (No 10418 Pte Markham H. and No 21396 Pte Eldreth T.W)	
		2 pm	Capt. T. O. Cook left the Company and joined No 96 Coy.	
	16th	8 pm	Sections 1 and 2 withdrawn to JEAN BART CAMP near COXYDE and arrived in camp at 2 am.	Dunkerque 1 a 10000
do	16th 17th		Situation calm except for intermittent shelling and counter battery work	
	18th		Situation calm except for counter battery work. Remaining two sections of Company relieved by No 199 M.G. Coy and on relief proceeded to JEAN BART CAMP. See O.O. No 18 No 3.	Appendix No 3.
	19th	2 am	Sections arrived JEAN BART CAMP 2 am without incident	
		1.30pm	Moved to Company GHYVELDE as per O.O No 19. arriving in billets at 5 pm.	Appendix No 4
	20th		Move to BRAY DUNES with 97th Infty Bgde arriving 10 am	Dunkerque 1a 100000

WAR DIARY

INTELLIGENCE SUMMARY

(Erase heading not required.)

Army Form C. 2118.

Place	Date	Hour	Summary of Events and Information	Remarks and references to Appendices
BRAY-DUNES	21st		Cleaning up and improving billets.	
"	22nd		Church parade and recreational training	
"	23rd 26th		Training as per training program	Appendix No 5
COXYDE	27th		Three and half sections relieved 96th M.G. Coy on coast defence work as per O.O. No 20. Relief completed 11.30 P.m. without incident	Appendix No 6
	28th 30th		Coast defence work.	
	31st		Two sections relieved by 199th M.G. Coy from coast defence work fare and proceeded to relieve two sections of 199 M.G. Coy in LOMBARTZYDE Sector. See O.O. No. 21 and 22	Appendices No 7 and No 8

COMDG. 219 COMPANY M.G. CORPS.
CAPT.

APPENDIX No. 1   OPERATION ORDER 16   30/6/17

Map refs sheet DUNKERQUE 1a 1/100000 sheet 12. S.W. 1/20000.

RELIEF
No. 3 and 4 sections of 219 Machine Gun Company will relieve two sections of 96 Machine Gun Company in the NIEUPORT area on the night July 1st/2nd and on completion of relief will come under the orders of G.O.C. 97 Inf. Bde.

ORDER OF BATTLE
No. 3 section under Lt J.W. Page Beard will relieve the section in the right of the sector. No. 4 section under Lt J.T. Allen will relieve the section in the left of the sector.

PARADE
Sections will parade at 5.45 pm complete with Transport. 1 Battle limber per section to parade.

ROUTE
No. 3 section will proceed via COXYDE - OOST DUNKERQUE to NIEUPORT to HQRS of 97 Machine Gun Company. No. 4 section will proceed via COXYDE - OOST - DUNKERQUE and 2nd class road through GROENEN-DYKE. Location HQRS No. 4 section M21.d.1.6 sheet 12. S.W. 1/20000.

DRESS
Fighting order.

EQUIPMENT
Guns complete with accessories and spare part boxes. 14 belt boxes per gun will be taken. No S.A.A. to be carried.

RATIONS
Rations for the 2-7-17 will be carried.

ADVANCE PARTY
Advance party consisting of one section officer and one sgt per section will proceed to NIEUPORT at 1.30 pm.

COMPLETION OF RELIEF
Completion of relief will be reported by section officer to HQRS 97 Machine Gun Company immediately the positions have been taken over and the guns installed.

ISSUED AT 10.45 pm
PLEASE ACKNOWLEDGE.

F.A. Hooper Lt.
COMDG. 219 COMPANY M.G. CORPS

Copy No. 7   OPERATION ORDER No. 17.   July 6

Map Refs. Nieuport 12 SW1 ed 1a 1/... Dunkerque 1a 1/100. APPDX No 2

RELIEF. An inter-Coy relief will take place on the evening of the 7th July 1917 – No 1 section will relieve No 4 Section in positions 5R 6R 7R 8R – No 2 Section will relieve No 3 section in positions 1R 2R 3R 4R on the Lombartzyde Sector. On completion of relief No 3 & 4 sections will return to Jean Bart Camp.

ROUTE. No 1 section will proceed via COXYDE – OOST DUNKERQUE – and 2nd class road through GROENEN-DYKE to HQrs No 4 section.
No 2 will proceed via COXYDE – OOST DUNKERQUE to NIEUPORT and report to HQ 97 MG Coy.

GUIDES. Guides for 1 2 3 4 positions will be at HQ 97th MG Coy at 7-30 pm and Guides for 5 6 7 8 positions at HQ No 4 section 7-30 pm.

PARADE. No 1 & 2 sections will parade at 5.45 pm

DRESS. Fighting Order.

TRANSPORT. 1 Battle Limber will parade with each section and will return with the Guns etc of the sections which have been relieved.

HANDING OVER. Guns Spare parts and Tripods only will be exchanged – Belt Boxes – S.A.A. Aiming Deflexes Overbank Mountings and any similar special equipment will be handed over to the relieving sections. Receipts will be obtained for all material handed over. Gun team commanders will see that all information in regard to gun positions is handed over to the incoming teams.

RATIONS. Rations for 8' will be carried by No 1 & 2 Sec

COMPLETION OF RELIEF. Completion of Relief will be reported to OC by word "BRANDY".

Issued at 10.45 am

Please ACKNOWLEDGE.

C. Hooper Lt.
COMDG. 219 COMPANY M.G. CORPS.

```
Copy No 1      SO No 1
      2          "  2
      3          "  3
      4          "  4
      5        Transport Off
      6        FILE.
      7        War Diary
      8          "
      9        OC 97th MG Coy
     10        Spare.
```

MG Coy

OPERATION ORDER No 18

SECRET   Map. Ref Nieuport 12 S.W.1

Appdx. No 3
July 17th 1917
Copy No. 5

RELIEF — 2 sections 219 MG Coy. will be relieved by 2 sections 199 MG Coy. in the subsector of LOMBARTZYDE on the night of 18/19th July.

EQUIPMENT — 14 Belt Boxes per gun team will be handed over to relieving sections, also all trench stores. All Guns, Tripods, spare parts, clinometers, and similar gun equipment will be removed on completion of relief. No Gun Tripod or equipment to be removed until incoming teams have taken over. Transport Officer will arrange to collect 112 belt boxes from 199 MG Coy at Jean Bart Camp by 4 pm 18/7/17.

GUIDES — One guide from HQ will be at M34 c 6-8 at 9 pm. No 3 section will have 3 guides at HQ at 9 pm. No 4 section, 1 guide at HQ at 9 pm and 3 guides at Ammtn Dump at 9-15 pm.

TRANSPORT — 2 complete Battle Limbers to be at HQ at 10 pm.

COMPLETION OF RELIEF — On completion of relief gun teams will proceed to HQ, pack its material on limbers and then proceed at 200 yd intervals to OOST DUNKIRK RAILWAY STATION when sections will form up and march to JEAN BART CAMP.

RECEIPTS — Section Officers will see that receipts are obtained for all stores handed over. Also receipts are obtained by each gun commander from incoming team.

PERSONNEL — 1 Officer and 3 OR will remain in the line for 24 hours after completion of relief, and will then proceed according to orders issued later.

ACKNOWLEDGE

Issued at 10 pm.

J.E. Hyde M.C. for Capt
Comdg. 219 Company M.G. Corps

Copy No 1 T.O.
    2 No 3 S.O.
    3 " 4 S.O.
    4 War Diary.
    5 War Diary.
    6 199 MG Coy.
    7 spare.

219 M.G. Coy   Operation Order No 19.   July 18' 1917

APPDX. No 4.

Ref Map Dunkerque 1/

Move — 219 M.G.Coy will move to Ghyvelde Area on the morning of July 19" 1917.

Route — La Panne – Adinkerke – Ghysbekvelde – Ghyvelde.

Parade — The transport will form up on the LaPanne – Coxcyde Road facing SW at 1-25 pm.

Sections will parade on road in front of their section limbers at 1-30 pm. All limbers to be packed by 11 am except Cooking Utensils.

Dress — Fighting Order. Packs to be packed on Battle Limbers. All water bottles to be filled.

Rations — The unconsumed portion of the days rations will be carried by the men.

March Discipline — will be strictly maintained. No man is to fall out without a chit from the OC Coy. Any man disregarding this order will be severely punished.

Billets — Lt S.L Vincent and 1 signaller will report to Area Commandant Ghyvelde not later than 11 am to arrange Billets.

Dinner — 11.45 am

Issued at 7 pm

J.M Hooper Lt.
COMDG. 219 COMPANY M.G. CORPS.

Copy   1   Off Mess
       2   CSM
       3   War Diary
       4
       5   File
       6   Spare

219 M.G.Coy
APPDX. N°5

TRAINING PROGRAMME for W.E. JULY 28th 1917.

Day	7-15 am – 7-45	9 a.m to 12 p.m	12 to 12-30 p.m.	2 to 3 p.m.	Remarks.
Mon Day	Physical Training.	Barrage Fire	Cleaning Guns.	Squad Drill with Arms.	During the Barrage Fire Parade the following points will be practised – selecting suitable positions – finding direction – placing out the Auxiliary aiming screen – Laying correctly and Neither raising and elevating dials. To be taught how to find direction without the assistance of an Officer. The method of maintaining Ammunition supply togten also be demonstrated.
Tues day.	Square Drill with Arms.	Preparation of hasty Emplacements.	Lecture by S/O's on Gas + Gas shells.	Physical Training under O.O. whilst this parade is in progress, since NCO of Section will be practised in the method of finding their positions on the map by resection.	
Wed.	Physical Training.	9 to 11.30 am Barrage Fire.	11-30 – 12-30 p.m. Box Respirator Drill.	Square Drill with Arms. Under Section Off. (During this Parade C.S.M. will lecture to ncos on "Discipline".)	
Thurs day	Square Drill with Arms.	N° 1/2 sect. Rangefinding N° 3/4 sect. Gun Drill from Pack Mules.	= Stoppages.	Cleaning Guns.	While firing on the range special attention to be paid to recovery of aim and regulation of fire. Men should be taught how to fire at varying rates of from 50 to 300 rounds per minute.
Fri day.	Physical Training.	N° 1/2 sect Gun Drill from Pack Mules N° 3/4 sect Rangefinding.	= Stoppages	Cleaning Guns.	Physical Training
			Cleaning Guns.	Square Drill with Arms	
				Cleaning Guns.	
Sat.	Square Drill with Arms	ROUTE MARCH		Lecture by S.O° on DISCIPLINE.	

signed W. Hooper Capt.
O.C. MG.219 COMPANY M.G. CORPS.

219 MG Coy   July 26th 1917

OPERATION ORDER No 20.   SECRET.

Map Ref Sheet 11 Belgium 1/40,000.   APPDX N°6

RELIEF. 3½ sections of 219 MG Coy will relieve 3½ sections of 96 MG Coy in Coast Defence work on July 27th and on completion of relief the Coy will come under the orders of 66th Div.

ORDER of BATTLE. No 3 section under 2Lt E.G. Lord will relieve the section in the Nieuport sector. No 1 section under 2Lt B.R. Edwards will relieve the section in the Oost Dunkirk sector. No 2 under Lt S.L. Vincent will relieve the section in the Coxyde sector. A sub-section of No 4 section under 2Lt J.R. Morley will relieve a subsection in the Ideswalde sector.

ROUTE. All sections will proceed via Adinkerke. Coxyde to CHQ at W.6.a.5.6.

GUIDES. 96 Coy will provide 1 guide per section at Coy HQ at 2 pm.

PARADE. Sections will parade on Coy Parade ground complete with Transport at 8.30 am. Limbers to be packed not later than 7-45.

DRESS. Fighting Order - Packs on - Limbers waterbottles - full -

EQUIPMENT. Guns complete with accessories, spare parts Boxes. 10 Belt Boxes per gun will be taken.

TAKING OVER. Section Officers are responsible that all information in regard to Emplacements, Standing Orders, Lines of Fire and any special instructions in regard to each position are carefully taken note of -

RATIONS. The unconsumed portion of the rations will be carried by the men. No 3 section will draw rations for 28th before leaving new HQ for gun positions.

COMPLETION of RELIEF will be reported by SO to new HQ by the word SHERRY - immediately the positions have been taken over and the guns installed. Transport will return to HQ Coxyde.

DISCIPLINE. All ranks are to be warned that positions occupied are such that they may receive a certain amount of Public attention and SO's are responsible for seeing that men are kept clean and well turned out.

BILLETS. SO's are responsible that all Billets are left in a clean condition and CSM will see that latrines are left in a proper state. One NCO and one man will be left behind to hand over Billets.

Reveille 5-30 am
Breakfast 6.0 am
Issued at 10 pm.

ACKNOWLEDGE.

F.A. Hooper, CAPT.
COMDG. 219 COMPANY M.G. CORPS.

219 M.G. Coy. July 31st/17

OPERATION ORDER No 21.

Appx 7

Relief. 2 sections of 219 M.G. Coy. will be relieved by 2 sections 199 Coy. from Coast Defence on the afternoon of July 31/17.

Guides. Guides to Gun Teams will be provided by S.O. at Rations Dumps at 9:30 pm.

Handing Over. All spare S.A.A. will be handed over, and section Officers are responsible that all Defence schemes and full particulars of Duties are made clear to incoming teams.

Completion of Relief. On completion of relief 2 sections will return to Coy HQrs Coxyde Bains and will then prepare to move into the Nieuport sector.

Acknowledge.
Issued at 1 pm

F.W. Hooker .... CAPT.
COMDG. 219 COMPANY M.G. CORPS.

Copy 1 OC No 1 sec
     2   " 2 "
     3 War Diary.
     4
     5 File.

219 M.G. Coy.   OPERATION ORDER No 22   July 31/1917
                                        APPDX 8

RELIEF. 2 sections of 219 Coy will relieve two sections of 199 Coy in the LOMBARTZYDE Sector on the night of July 31st/Aug 1st.

ORDER of Battle. No 1 section under 2nd Lt B.R. Edwards will be on the left and No 2 section under 2nd Lt B.R. Edwards will be on the right.

Guides Gun teams will be met at the HQrs of 199 Coy Nieuport at 9.30 pm.

Parades The 2 sections will parade at 8 pm complete with transport (one limber per section) and will proceed to HQ at intervals of at least 100 yds between sections.

Equipments Guns, Tripods, Spare Parts and 14 Belt Boxes per gun will be carried on limbers. No SAA to be taken into the trenches.

Gas. When marching through Nieuport and in the line special precautions must be taken against Gas. The enemy are mixing Gas shells with High Explosive and whenever a Bombardment is commenced Gas helmets will be donned immediately. Helmets will not be removed without permission from an officer or responsible NCO.

Completion of Relief will be advised by word "KUMMEL" sent to CHQ immediately the position have been taken over.

ACKNOWLEDGE

Issued at 1 pm.

J.F. Allin
Lieut for CAPT.
COMDG. 219 COMPANY M.G. CORPS.

Copy 1 SO No 1
     2   " No 2
     3 199 M.G. Coy
     4 T.O.
     5 War Diary
     6   "   "
     7 File.

Confidential.   Original.

WAR DIARY.
of
219th MACHINE GUN Coy.

Volume 6.

From August 1st 1917.   To August 31st 1917.

Vol 6

Army Form C. 2118.

WAR DIARY
or
INTELLIGENCE SUMMARY

(Erase heading not required.)

Instructions regarding War Diaries and Intelligence Summaries are contained in F. S. Regs., Part II. and the Staff Manual respectively. Title pages will be prepared in manuscript.

Place	Date	Hour	Summary of Events and Information	Remarks and references to Appendices
NIEUPORT	August 1st	12.30 am	Relief completed. During the relief NIEUPORT shelled heavily and one half limber destroyed by direct hit and No 2/120 Dr Thompson J killed.	
do	2nd		Situation normal during day. During night sensitive points fired on with indirect fire and 6025 rounds expended from gun positions at approx M28 C.17	NIEUPORT 12.S.W Edition 2A
do	3rd/4th		Indirect fire carried out throughout day and night and on sensitive points. Particularly LOMBARTZYDE. 4000 rounds expended. At about 4pm enemy shelled our front and second lines very heavily for about 30 minutes	do
do	5th		ditto. 6400 rounds fired. Enemy retaliated heavily and No 3802 Sgt. T. Hollingsworth distinguished himself by digging out a number of Infantry men buried in a dugout near M 28. C. 17 whilst the shelling was in progress. He subsequently was gassed and evacuated. For his gallant action he received the Military Medal.	do
do	6th		Harassing fire carried out throughout day and night from M28 C. 3.7 on LOMBARTZYDE and M.16 Bos. 47 -6000 rounds fired. Enemy retaliation slight.	do
do	7th		Harassing fire throughout day and night on LOMBARTZYDE and M.16 b. 05. 47 - 3000 rounds fired.	do

Army Form C. 2118.

WAR DIARY
INTELLIGENCE SUMMARY.
(Erase heading not required.)

Instructions regarding War Diaries and Intelligence Summaries are contained in F. S. Regs., Part II. and the Staff Manual respectively. Title pages will be prepared in manuscript.

Place	Date	Hour	Summary of Events and Information	Remarks and references to Appendices
NIEUPORT	8th August	1 am to 4 am	Cooperated with Infantry 6 West Ridings in raid and fired 1800 rounds on sensitive points in LOMBARTZYDE, M.19.c.15.17 that M.18.d.4.85. Raid was successful and resulted in capture of 5 prisoners and a machine gun. Retaliation slight. Objective of raid M.12.b. at M.12.b.55.40.	NIEUPORT 12 S.W Edition 2A
do		10pm -11pm	Harassing fire on sensitive points – 2000 rounds	do
do	9th	1.30 am - 4 am	Cooperated in a projector and Stokes mortar gas attack on LOMBARTZYDE and GROOT BAMBURGH FARM. Indirect fire from M.28.c.5.17, M.28.a.65.95 and M.21.d.55.65 on M.19.c.15.50 – d.60.96. and LOM BARTZYDE 43000 rounds fired – Retaliation slight – no casualties	do
		10 am - 1 pm	Harassing fire on sensitive points 4500 rounds. Shelling normal	
		9 pm	No 2 Section relieved by No 3 Section – Relief completed 9 pm – no casualties	
do	10th	3 am - 12 pm	Harassing fire throughout day and night on sensitive points. 1600 rounds fired. Enemy put down a barrage at about 10 p.m. to which our artillery replied and all machine guns fired on S.O.S lines. The enemy knocked out two M.g. emplacements, one at M.28.c. art. wounding No 30159 Sgt W. McKeown and No 61309 Pte Stephens R.T. (who died of wounds) and one at M.28.d.5.65 wounding 2/Lt B.R. EDWARDS.	NIEUPORT. 12 S.W Edition 2A

Army Form C. 2118.

WAR DIARY
INTELLIGENCE SUMMARY
(Erase heading not required.)

Instructions regarding War Diaries and Intelligence Summaries are contained in F. S. Regs., Part II. and the Staff Manual respectively. Title pages will be prepared in manuscript.

Place	Date	Hour	Summary of Events and Information	Remarks and references to Appendices
NIEUPORT	Aug. 11th	8.a.m -5 p.m	Harassing fire throughout day on sensitive points 4000 rounds fired	8 a.m
		9 p.m	Relieved by 14th M.G. Coy - see O.O. N° 23. Relief completed at 11 p.m and sections arrived JEAN BART camp 2.a.m. No unusual shelling and no casualties	Appendix N° 1 / 9 p.m
COXYDE	12th		Cleaning up and kit inspections	8 a.m
do	13th		Training parades - especially Barrage drill	8 a.m
do	14th		do.	8 a.m
BRAY DUNES	15th		March from COXYDE to BRAY DUNES as per O.O. N° 24. Company arrived in Camp. 1.30 p.m	Appendix N° 2 / 8 a.m

Army Form C. 2118.

WAR DIARY

INTELLIGENCE SUMMARY.

(Erase heading not required.)

Instructions regarding War Diaries and Intelligence Summaries are contained in F. S. Regs., Part II. and the Staff Manual respectively. Title pages will be prepared in manuscript.

Place	Date	Hour	Summary of Events and Information	Remarks and references to Appendices
BRAY-DUNES	Aug 16. to 18th		Training as per training program	See Appendix No 3
do	19th		Inspection Parade and recreational training	do
do	20th to 25th		Training as per training program	See Appendix No 4
do	26th		Inspection Parade and recreational training	do
COXYDE	27th		Move from Bray Dunes to Australia Camp Coxyde. Move completed by 6 p.m. Company bivouaced for the night. See O.O No. 25. One subsection of No 2 under 2/Lt. Wright to Oost acentral on anti-aircraft work.	See Appendix No 5. Oost-Dunkerque Sheet 11 1/40000
do	28th		Move from bivouacs into huts in Australia Camp. No 4 Section under 2/Lt Morley proceeded to line to relieve one section 248 M.S.Coy - See O.O No 26 Relief Completed without undue shelling by 10 p.m.	See Appendix No 6.

WAR DIARY

Army Form C. 2118.

Instructions regarding War Diaries and Intelligence Summaries are contained in F. S. Regs., Part II. and the Staff Manual respectively. Title pages will be prepared in manuscript.

(Erase heading not required.)

Place	Date	Hour	Summary of Events and Information	Remarks and references to Appendices
COXYDE	26th		One Subsection No 3 under 2/Lt Maxwell proceeded to Bouave Road to relieve one subsection 248 M.G. Coy on anti-aircraft work. See O.O No 24.	Appendix No 7
do	27th	9 am	Subsection at '71' a central relieved by Infantry with Lewis guns.	for Oost Dunkerque Sheet 11 1/40000
do		12 noon to 6 pm	Enemy shelled Australia Camp intermittently throughout day and caused several casualties amongst other units.	full
do		12 pm	Gun of No 4 Section at approx M3d 4.9 cooperated with Infantry opening fire on a pre-arranged signal and did good work in assisting to repel enemy raid on one of our Posts.	Trench map no 5 1/10000
do	30th	-	Dispositions unchanged. Reserve lines behind Nieuport reconnoitred for gun positions.	far
do	31st		Dispositions unchanged. Work on new emplacement in M13d 1.1. commenced.	Map Ry Nieuport 17 S.W.

CAPT.
COMDG. 219 COMPANY M.G. CORPS.

SECRET.

August 10/17.

Appendix No 4

OPERATION ORDER No. 23.

Reference map DUNKERQUE. 1ᴬ 1/100000.

1. RELIEF. The 219th M. G. Coy - less two sections - will be relieved by the 14th M. G. Co, less two sections, in the LOMBARTZYDE sector during the evening of August 11th 1917 and will on completion of relief march to JEAN BART CAMP.

2. GUIDES. One guide per section will be at Company H.Q NIEUPORT. at 7.45 pm.

3. HANDING OVER

All trench stores, emplacements dug-outs etc will be handed over in a clean and proper condition and receipts will be obtained from incoming sections to this effect.

Belt boxes - 14 per gun - and all S.A.A will also be handed over. Section Officers are responsible for seeing that all defence schemes and lines of fire are fully understood by incoming officers and that any special information in regard to emplacements and works on hand is properly handed over.

Anti - Aircraft positions and all Anti - Aircraft equipment will be handed over and receipts obtained.

TRANSPORT.

One complete limber will be at Coy. H.Q NIEUPORT at 8.30 pm. If the town is being heavily shelled the limber will not enter NIEUPORT, but will wait on the ZOUAVE ROAD about 100ˣ from NIEUPORT.

COMPLETION OF RELIEF.

On completion of relief sections will proceed by Gun Teams, to the limber (No 2. section will pack their material on the front half. No 1. section theirs on the rear half) and will immediately proceed in Subsections at 100ˣ interval to JEAN BART CAMP. No 1 section will detail a brakesman.

Section officers will report relief complete to C.H.Q by word "THANKFUL" after their sections are clear of the trenches.

6. Rear HQ will make arrangements to provide a hot meal for sections on arrival at JEAN BART CAMP.

[signature] Hooper
CAPT.
COMDG. 219 COMPANY M.G. CORPS.

ACKNOWLEDGE.

Issued at 6 pm.

COPY. Nº 1.   S.O. Nº 1
  "   " 2.   S.O. " 3
  "   " 3.   TRANSPORT
  "   " 4.   4ᵗʰ M.G. Coy.

219th MG Coy.   SECRET   August 14/17

Operation Order No 24.

Appendix No 2

Map Reference — Dunkerque 1a

MOVE. 219 MG Coy less one subsection will move from Australia Camp to Bray Dunes Area on the morning of the 15th August.

ORDER of MARCH. HQrs — No 1 Section with section transport, followed by No 2 & 3 sections in similar formation — subsection of No 4 Section with two limbers — HQ limber — Water Cart — Mess Cart. Interval of 30 yards between Sections. The guard will march with HQrs.

DRESS. Fighting Order — Packs to be carried on limbers.

PARADE. Coy will parade under Section arrangmts. to be on the COXYDE - LA PANNE Rd facing S W at.

MARCH DISCIPLINE. March Discipline must be strictly maintained. No man is allowed to fall out on the line of march without a chit from OC Coy. Any man disregarding this order is liable to a Courtmartial. Brakesmen must not hang on to the back of limbers and nothing whatsoever is to be put on the Watercart.

OFFICERS CHARGERS. to be fully equipped and to carry feeds, water buckets, head ropes, picketing ropes and spare shoes. Only regulation bridles to be worn.

BILLETS. Section Officers are responsible for leaving Billets in a clean condition and will report this to OC Coy by. Officers are individually responsible that their own billets are left scrupulously clean. The CSM will see that Latrines are closed by

LIMBERS will be packed by 8 am with the exception of cooking utensils which will be on the limbers not later than 8.30 am

RATIONS. The unconsumed portion of the days rations will be carried by the men and rations for 16 on the G.S. wagon.

Reveille 6.0 am.
Breakfast 7.0 am.

ACKNOWLEDGE.

Issued at 7.30 pm
Copy No 1 OC no 1 sec
    2   "   2.
    3   "   3.
    4   "   4.

Copy No 5
    6 War Diary
    7
    8 File.

N Hooper CAPT.
COMDG 219 COMPANY M.G. CORPS.

Appendix No 3.

219. M.G.Coy.

Training Programme.

Date	6.30 – 7.30	8.30 to 9.30	9.30 to 12.30	2 to 3pm
Thurs 16.	P.T.	Squad Drill with arms.	No 1/2 section Firing Stoppages. No 3/4 section Barrage Drill.	Cleaning Limbers and guns and Refilling Belts.
Friday 17.	P.T.	Squad Drill with arms.	No 1/2 section Barrage Drill. No 3/4 section Firing Stoppages.	Cleaning Guns and Limbers and Belt filling.
18.	P.T.	Squad Drill with arms.	1/2 section Practise H+G scheme for Barrage. 3/4 section Barrage Drill.	Cleaning Limbers & equipment.

W. Hooper. CAPT.
COMDG. 219 COMPANY M.G. CORPS.

Appendix "04"

219 MG Coy — TRAINING PROGRAMME for week ending AUGUST 25" 1917

	6.30–7.30	8.30 to 9.30	9.30 am to 10.15am	10.30 am to 11.30 pm	2 pm to 3.30	5.15 – 6.30	Remarks
MON 20TH	P.T.	Arms Drill.	Elementary Gun Drill.	Use of Auxiliary Aiming Screen.	Care & Cleaning Spare Parts.	Lecture by S.O. to NCOs on map reading including use of compass and "How to find the Enemy".	1) P.T. to include running with Guns and Tripods. 2) Kites to be utilised as targets for instruction in use of Aeroplane Sights.
TUES 21ST	P.T.	Square Drill including Saluting Drill.	Elementary Gun Drill.	Laying guns for Direction (a) by map and compass. (b) by map, R.O. and direction dial.	2pm to 3pm Aeroplane Sights. 3–3.30 pm Care & Cleaning.		
WED 22ND	P.T.	Arms Drill.	Combined Drill.	Use of Aeroplane Sights.	Coy Sports.		
THURS 23RD	P.T.	Square Drill including Saluting Drill.	One-Man Gun Drill.	Barrage Drill including use of Cam Screen and Laying gun for direction.	Tactical handling of Machine Guns including making of hasty emplacements.	Lecture by S.O. to NCOs on "The employment of Machine Guns in the attack".	
FRI 24TH	P.T.	Arms Drill.	Practical Demonstration of Barrage Drill with ball ammunition firing out to Sea.		Tactical handling (as above)		
SAT 25TH	P.T.	Square Drill including Saluting Drill.	Pack Transport Drill to include loading Pack Animals from Limbers and Action from Pack Animals &c.		Immediate Action firing Ball Ammunition wearing Box Respirators.	Lecture by S.O. to NCOs on "Fire Direction".	

219 MG Coy.   Appendix No 5.
                                                     August 28/..

OPERATION ORDER No 25

Move. 219 MG Coy will move from Bray Dunes to Australia Camp during 27th inst.

Order of March HQrs No 1 section with section transport followed by No 2, 3, 4 sections in similar formation. HQrs limber, Water Cart, Mess Cart. Interval of 30 yds between sections. The guard will march with HQrs.

Dress Fighting Order. Packs to be carried on limbers.

Parade Coy will parade under section arrangements to be on the Byroad facing south at 1-45 pm. Transport to be hooked in at 12-45 pm and to be on the road not later than 1-30 pm.

March Discipline March Discipline must be strictly maintained. No man is allowed to fall out on the line of march without a chit from OC Coy. Any man disregarding this order is liable to a Court Martial. Brakesmen must not hang on to the back of limbers.

Officers Chargers. To be fully equipped with feeds, water buckets, head ropes, picketing ropes and spare shoes. Only regulation bridles to be worn.

Billets. SO are responsible that Billets are left in a clean condition and will report this to OC Coy by 1-30 pm. Officers will also see that their own billets are clean. CSM will see that all latrines are properly left.

Limbers Limbers will be packed by 11am except Cooking utensils.

Rations The unconsumed portion of the day's rations will be carried by the men.

Dinner 12 o'clock.

Acknowledge

Issued at 8 am.

                                    W. Hooker Capt.
                                    COMDG. 219 COMPANY M.G. CORPS.

        Copy No 1   OC No 1
             2   " 2
             3   " 3
             4   " 4
             5   TO
             6   File
             7   War Diary
             8
             9   Spare

Secret.

Operation Order No 26
Map reference: Nieuport SW

Aug 28/1917
Appendix No 6

Relief: One section of 219 M.G. Coy will relieve one section of 248 M.G. Coy in the LOMBARTZYDE SECTOR on the night of Aug 28/29'- 1917.

Parade: No 4 section under 2nd Lt R J Morley will parade at 5.15 pm.

Dress: Fighting Order.

Transport: 5 pack animals will be provided to carry guns equipment & rations.

Taking Over: Only Guns Tripods & Spare Parts Boxes will be taken into the line. Belt Boxes S.A.A. & Night Screws etc to be taken over from the Coy which is being relieved.

Rations: The unconsumed portion of the Days Rations will be carried by the men and rations for 29' will be carried on the pack animals.

H dqtrs: will remain at Australian Camp. Morning Reports and important information will be sent to HQtrs 14 M.G. Coy Nieuport.

Completion of Relief: To be reported by runner to Coy HQtrs by word "DUNKIRK".

Acknowledge

Issued at 4 pm

(signed) Ta Hooper CAPT.
OOMDG. 219 COMPANY M.G. CORPS.

Copy No 1 OC No 4 sec.
        2 T.O.
        3 War Diary
        4 "   "
        5 File.

Secret   August 28/1917

Operation Order No 27.   Appendix No. 7.
Map ref Dunkirk 1.a/.

Relief:-   One subsection of 219 M/Coy will relieve one subsection of 248 M/Coy on Anti Aircraft work in positions on the Zouave Road during afternoon of Aug 28/1917

Taking Over.   No Belt Boxes and no A.A. sights will be taken over —

Parade.   One subsection of No 3 section under 2/Lt G.B. Maxwell to parade at 2.30 pm complete with one limber.

Completion of Relief to be reported to HQrs by word "Active" —

Acknowledge.
Issued at 12.30 pm

                                     J.A. Hooper CAPT.
                                     COMDG. 219 COMPANY M.G. CORPS.

Copy No 1   2/Lt G.B. Maxwell
         2   T.O.
         3   War Diary
         4   "   "
         5   File.

CONFIDENTIAL

WAR DIARY

of

219 MACHINE GUN COY

Volume 7.

From September 1st 1917.

To September 30th 1917.

Army Form C. 2118.

WAR DIARY

INTELLIGENCE SUMMARY

(Erase heading not required.)

Place	Date	Hour	Summary of Events and Information	Remarks and references to Appendices
NIEUPORT	Sept 1st		Dispositions unchanged. 3500 rounds fired from M21d on M22.a.13.52 & M21.b.89.70 and M21.b.89.70 & M21.b.85.70 to repel enemy attempt to rush our post.	NIEUPORT 1/5.w. Appendix No. 1.
do	2nd	2 pm	No 5 subsection relieved No 6 subsection on anti-aircraft duties on Zouave Road as per O.O No 28. Relief completed by 5 pm without undue occurrence.	do No 2
		5 pm	No 1 Section relieved No 4 Section in the LOMBARTZYDE sector. Relief completed by 10 pm. Shelling normal - no casualties. See O.O No 29.	
do	3rd 4th		Dispositions unchanged.	
do	5th		Dispositions unchanged. At about 9 pm enemy aeroplanes dropped bombs on rest billets at COXYDE obtaining two direct hits on a hut occupied by the sections resting - killing two men and wounding 30 of whom four subsequently died of wounds. No 31147 Pte Hill A. and No 30715 Sgt Robinson J. and No 29719 Sgt Barons distinguished themselves by the manner in which they rendered aid to the wounded without consideration of their own danger. The former was subsequently awarded the Military Medal (16.9.17) and the two latter received Gallantry Cards. (15.9.17)	
do	6th		Dispositions unchanged. M21.d PREFOUE-IL. was shelled with S.g's inter-mittenly throughout night.	NIEUPORT 1/5.w.

Army Form C. 2118.

WAR DIARY
INTELLIGENCE SUMMARY.
(Erase heading not required.)

Instructions regarding War Diaries and Intelligence Summaries are contained in F. S. Regs., Part II. and the Staff Manual respectively. Title pages will be prepared in manuscript.

Place	Date	Hour	Summary of Events and Information	Remarks and references to Appendices
NIEUPORT	7th Sept.		Subsection No1 Section under 2/Lt W. Wright occupied two gun positions at approx M.29 b.7.65 for close defence work. Completed by 10 p.m. without unusual occurrence.	Nieuport 12.S.W.
do			Remaining dispositions unchanged. Shelling normal	do
do	8th	3.15 am – 5 am	During night the positions at M.29.d were subjected to an intense bombardment by S.G.'s, 4.2's whizzbangs and gas shells, and as result several direct hits were obtained on emplacements and five men were wounded gassed. In addition No 29572 Cpl. Johnson was accidentally wounded the concussion of a bursting shell knocking him off the parapet on to a bayonet standing in the trench.	do
do	9th		No 3 Section under 2/Lt J. Goldman relieved No 1 Section in positions at M.29.d, one subsection of No 1 taking over anti-aircraft duties at Zouave Road on being relieved. All reliefs completed and teams in new positions by 12 p.m.	do
do	10th		Dispositions unchanged. Enemy artillery active all day particularly in neighborhood of M.29 b.7.6.	do
do	11th / 13		Dispositions unchanged. Situation normal	do

Army Form C. 2118.

WAR DIARY

~~INTELLIGENCE SUMMARY.~~

(Erase heading not required.)

Instructions regarding War Diaries and Intelligence Summaries are contained in F. S. Regs., Part II. and the Staff Manual respectively. Title pages will be prepared in manuscript.

Place	Date	Hour	Summary of Events and Information	Remarks and references to Appendices
NIEUPORT	14th		Subsection on anti-aircraft duty relieved by subsection of 4th M.G. Coy. as per O.O. No 30. Relief completed by 5 p.m.	Appendix No 3.
do		5 a.m.	Gun positions at M 21 d shelled heavily and two men wounded, one of whom subsequently died. No 25114 Pte W Morvan distinguished himself by going alone three times through the hostile barrage to obtain stretcher and in helping the wounded back. To do this it was necessary to pass along a narrow strip of land about 3 yards wide. For his conduct on this occasion he subsequently received the Military Medal.	
do	15th / 16th		Dispositions unchanged. Enemy shelling normal.	
do	17th / 18th / 19th		Reliefs as per Operation order No 31. All carried out without any unusual occurrence or undue hostile shelling	Appendix No 4.
do	20th		Subsection on anti-aircraft duty relieved by subsection of 4th M.G.Coy. as per O.O. No 35. Relief completed by 5 p.m.	Appendix No 1.

Army Form C. 2118.

WAR DIARY
INTELLIGENCE SUMMARY

(Erase heading not required.)

Place	Date	Hour	Summary of Events and Information	Remarks and references to Appendices
NIEUPORT	Sept 24th/25th		Dispositions unchanged. Normal hostile shelling and aerial activity.	
do	25th	9pm	Subsection No 3 relieved subsection No 1 in BRIQUETTERIE. Relief completed 9.30 pm without incident. See operation order No 28.	Appendix No 6
do	26th	4pm	Co-operation with artillery in concentration on LOMBARTZYDE Sector. Two guns in BRIQUETTERIE fired 600 rounds on enemy front line at Mnt A.U.15 and d.7.8. Retaliation on gun positions very slight.	4 guns
		9pm	No 2 Section relieved No 1 Section in PRESQU'ILE. Slight hostile shelling and machine gun fire during relief which was completed at 10 pm. No casualties. See operation order No 33.	do 4 guns
do	27th	6 am	Two guns in BRIQUETTERIE and two guns in PRESQU'ILE fired on S.O.S. 1500 rounds fired. Both positions shelled slightly without effect.	4 guns
do	28th/29th	2pm	Three guns of No 1 Section relieved three guns of 91 M.G. Coy on anti-aircraft work in COXYDE area. Relief complete by 4 pm. O.O. No 34	NIEUPORT 17.S.W. Appendix No 7 4 guns
			Dispositions unchanged.	4 guns

Army Form C. 2118.

WAR DIARY

INTELLIGENCE SUMMARY.

(Erase heading not required.)

Instructions regarding War Diaries and Intelligence Summaries are contained in F. S. Regs., Part II. and the Staff Manual respectively. Title pages will be prepared in manuscript.

Place	Date	Hour	Summary of Events and Information	Remarks and references to Appendices
NIEUPORT	Sept 30th	10 am	No 1 Section on Anti aircraft work relieved by three guns of 96th M.G. Coy as per O.O No 35. Relief complete by 12 noon.	Appendix No 8
		6.30 pm	Subsection No 4 relieved by two Lewis guns of 14th Bde from anti-aircraft work and proceeded to occupy positions at M35 c.20.90 as per O.O No 36. Relief completed without incident	Appendix No 9
		11 pm	Gun positions M.3.d shelled lightly - resulting in two casualties (wounds)	Nieuport N.W.

SECRET.   Appendix No 1   Appendix No 1.

OPERATION ORDER No 28.
Ref Map DUNKIRK 1a.

September 2nd 1917.

RELIEF.
No 5. Subsection of 219 M.G Coy. will relieve No. 6. subsection on Anti Aircraft work in positions on the Zouave Road. during the afternoon of Sept. 3rd 1917.

TAKING OVER.
Guns and all Equipment will be taken over by the ingoing subsection.

PARADE.
No 5. Subsection under 2/Lt. J.W. Goldman will parade at 2.30 p.m. complete with one limber.

COMPLETION OF RELIEF.
To be reported to Coy HQ by 2/Lt. G.B. Maxwell.

M. Hooker, CAPT.
COMDG. 219 COMPANY M.G. CORPS.

ACKNOWLEDGE...
ISSUED AT.... 2-30 p.m.

Copy. No 1. 2/Lt. Goldman
 "   " 2. 2/Lt. Maxwell.
 "   " 3. T.O.
 "   " 4. War Diary
 "   " 5.   "   "
 "   " 6. File.

Secret Appendix No 2 Sept 2/1917

Operation Order No 29
Ref. Map Nieuport 12.S.W.

Relief: No. 1 section will relieve No 4 section of 219 M.G. Coy in the Lombartzyde Sector on the night of 3/4th September 1917

Parade: No. 1 section under Lt 7 Abbott will parade at 5.15 pm.

Dress: Fighting Order.

Transport: 3 pack animals will be provided to carry guns, equipment, and rations.

Taking Over: Only Guns and spare parts will be taken. Tripods, Belt-Boxes, S.A.A., screens etc will be taken over from No 4 section.

Rations: The unconsumed portion of the days rations will be carried by the men and rations for 4th will be carried by the pack animals.

HQrs will remain at Australia Camp.

Reports: Reports and important information will be sent to HQrs 14 M.G. Coy Nieuport. A daily report will be sent to Coy HQrs by rations carriers each night.

Completion of Relief: O.C. No. 1 will report that relief has been carried out.

Acknowledge
Issued at 3pm.

F.C. Harcourt Lucy Lt. CAPT.
COMDG. 219 COMPANY M.G. CORPS.

Copy 1 OC No 1
     2 " " 1
     3 T.O.
     4 War Diary
     5 File
     6 File

219 M.G.Coy.   Appendix No 3   SECRET.

OPERATION ORDER No 30
Map Ref. RAMSCAPELLE 12-S.W.3.

September 14·17

RELIEF. The Sub section of 219th M.G.Coy. on A.A. Defence at 3 Kings Farm will be relieved by Sub section of 14th M.G.Coy.
Relief to be completed by 6 p.m.

GUIDES Guides for positions will be at "Three Kings Farm" at 3 p.m.

EQUIPMENT Guns, Tripods, Spare parts and all equipment will be brought out.

HANDING OVER Handing over certificates to be made out in triplicate and signed by both officers concerned 2/Lieut Smith will hand relief complete certificate and one copy of handing over certificate to Orderly Room 14th M.G.Coy Hut 41 Australia Camp as soon as possible after relief. The remaining copy of above to be handed to Orderly Room 219th M.G.Coy.

ISSUED AT

ACKNOWLEDGE.

CAPT
COMDG. 219 COMPANY M.G. CORPS

219. M.G. Coy.   Appendix No 4   SECRET.
                                   Sept 16th 1917.
OPERATION ORDER No 31.
                                   COPY No. 9
Map. NIEUPORT. sheet 12 S W 1/10000

RELIEF.

An intercompany relief will take place on the nights of Sept. 17/18th and 18/19th as follows:-

(a) One subsection of No 4 Section under 2Lt Morley will relieve one subsection of No 2. Section in the BRIQUETTERIE on the night Sept 17/18th.

(b) No 1. Section under 2/Lt F.C. Smith will relieve No 3. Section in the PRESQUE-IL on the night Sept. 18/19th.

PARADES.

Relieving section will parade under section arrangements, at 5.30 p.m.

DRESS.

Fighting order. Water bottles to be filled

TRANSPORT.

Pack animals to be provided to carry rations and gun equipment - to parade at 5. p.m.

TAKING OVER.

Spare parts only to be exchanged. Guns and all other equipment to be handed over to incoming teams. All information regarding positions, lines of fire etc., to be made perfectly clear to relieving sections.

RATIONS.

Unconsumed portion of days rations to be carried on the man, and rations for the following day to be carried on pack mules. Animals to wait for outgoing teams to carry spare parts etc.

HEADQUARTERS.

Advanced Company HQRS. will be opened at 95. Rue Longue. NIEUPORT. at 10.a.m. Sept. 17th all reports to be sent to advanced HQRS.

COMPLETION OF RELIEF.

To be reported to C.H.Q. by word "HAPPY". On completion of relief the outgoing teams will proceed to C.H.Q. at AUSTRALIA CAMP.

ISSUED AT
ACKNOWLEDGE.
                                        CAPT.
                            COMDG. 219 COMPANY M.G. CORPS.

            COPY. No 1   Headquarters
               "   No 2   O.C. No 1 Section
               "   3   "   " 2   "
               "   4   "   " 3   "
COPY. No 8/9 WAR DIARY.
               "   5   "   " 4   "
               "   6   Transport officer
               "   7   O.C. 96. MGC. (For information)

219 M.G Coy.   Appendix 5.   SECRET.

OPERATION ORDER No 32
Map Ref. RAMSCAPELLE 12. S.W.3.

RELIEF.
No. 2. Sub section 219th M.G. Coy. will relieve Sub. section of 14 M.G. Coy. on A.A. at "THREE KINGS FARM." on the morning September 20th. Relief to be completed by 6 pm.

GUIDES.
Guides to positions will be at "THREE KINGS FARM." at 10.30 am.

EQUIPMENT
Guns. Tripods. A.A. sights and spare part boxes will be carried. Belt boxes and S.A.A will be taken over from the outgoing Company.

TRANSPORT.
One half limber will parade at 9.35 am. After relief is completed this half limber will carry the equipment of the relieved Sub-section and return same to 14 M.G. Coy AUSTRALIA CAMP

PARADE
The Sub section will parade in Fighting order at 10 am.

HANDING OVER
Certificates to be made out in Triplicate and signed by both officers concerned. One copy to be retained by each Officer and the Other to be returned to ORDERLY ROOM. 219th M.G. Coy.

RATIONS.
Unconsumed portion of days. rations to be carried on man.

COMPLETION OF RELIEF.
Completion of relief to be reported by Word "NESSIE".

ISSUED AT 6. pm.
ACKNOWLEDGE.

COPY No 5.

COPY	No 1	HQRS
"	" 2	No 2. Section.
"	" 3.	TRANSPORT OFFICER
"	" 4.	14 M G COY
"	" 5	WAR DIARY.
"	" 6	" "
"	" 7	FILE.

SECRET   APPENDIX No 6   23rd September
219 M.G. Coy.

OPERATION ORDER No 33
Map ref. NIEUPORT 12.S.W 1/20000
RAMSCAPELLE 12 S.W 3 1/20000

COPY No. 9

RELIEF.
An intercompany relief will take place on the nights of Sept. 25th/26th and 26th/27th as follows:—

Sept. 25th/26th. Subsection of No 3 section under 2/Lt Maxwell will relieve subsection of No 4 section in the BRIQUETTERIE. On relief subsection of No 4 will proceed to THREE KINGS FARM and on the morning of the 26th take over the "Anti Aircraft duties" from subsection of No 2 Section.

Sept 26th/27th No 2 Section under 2/Lt E.G. Ford and 2/Lt Wright will relieve No 1 section in the PRESQU'IL. On completion of relief No 1 section will proceed to AUSTRALIA CAMP.

PARADES
Sections will parade at 5 p.m. in Fighting Order.
On the 26th/27th subsection of No 2 Section from AUSTRALIA CAMP will proceed via "Three Kings Farm" and will there be joined by subsection under 2/Lt Wright. Men to march in single file and an interval of not less than 50' to be maintained between Gun Teams.

EQUIPMENT.
Spare Parts only will be exchanged. All Guns, Tripods, Ammunition etc will be handed over to incoming teams.

HANDING OVER
Section Officers are responsible that the handing over is carried out correctly in every detail and that all schemes and special features of each emplacement are made clear to incoming teams.

TRANSPORT
Pack animals required will parade at 5 p.m. on each day.

RATIONS.
Unconsumed portion of days rations to be carried on the men. Rations for following day to be carried on Pack animals.

COMPLETION OF RELIEF
To be reported to ADV. H.Q by word "BRUNER" by outgoing teams.

W. Hooper CAPT:
COMDG. 219 COMPANY M.G. CORPS.

ISSUED AT 1.30 p.m.
PLEASE ACKNOWLEDGE.

COPY No 1   HQRS
    "   2   LT LOTT ADV. H.Q
    "   3   O.C. No 1 SECTION
    "   4   O.C. " 2 "
    "   5   O.C. " 3 "
    "   6   O.C. " 4 "
    "   7   LT. WRIGHT
    "   8   LIEUT. ALLEN
    "   9/10 WAR DIARY

SECRET   Appendix No 7   SEPTEMBER 26. 1917

OPERATION ORDER No 34
Map. Ref. DUNKERQUE 1A 1/100000

Copy No 4

RELIEF.
No. 1 Section 219th M.G.Coy. (less One gun team) under 2/Lt Smith will relieve 3 Guns of 97th M.G.Coy. on ANTI AIRCRAFT defence on the 27th September in the COXYDE area.

PARADE.
Section will parade at 1.15pm. Dress fighting Order.

GUIDES.
One guide per Gun team will be at H.Q. 97th M.G.C. AUSTRALIA CAMP at 1.30pm.

EQUIPMENT.
Guns, Tripods, Spare parts and Anti Aircraft sights to be taken. Belt boxes will be handed over by outgoing teams.

TRANSPORT
Three pack animals to parade at 12.45pm. to carry equipment.

RATIONS.
Unconsumed portion of days rations to be carried by the men.

COMPLETION OF RELIEF.
Completion of relief to be reported to C.H.Q by word 'NORA'.

             T.A. Hooper .... CAPT.
             COMDG. 219 COMPANY M.G. CORPS.

ISSUED AT 9pm.
ACKNOWLEDGE.

COPY. No 1. HQRS.
" " 2 O.C No 1. Section
" " 3 97th M.G. Coy.
" " H/S WAR DIARY
" " 6. FILE.
" " 7. Transport

SECRET Appendix No. 8

OPERATION ORDER No 35.
Map Ref. COXYDE 1/20000.

COPY No 5

RELIEF.
No 1 Section 219th M.G. Coy. less one Gun team, will be relieved by three Guns of 96th M.G. Coy. on Anti-Aircraft defence on the morning of September 30th 1917 in the following positions
      X 8. b. 2. 4
      X 13. C. 45. 25
      N 13. a. 65. 10

GUIDES.
One guide from each position will be at the entrance to AUSTRALIA CAMP. at 10 am.

TRANSPORT
Three pack animals will parade at 10. am to transport Guns etc to camp.

EQUIPMENT
Guns, Tripods, anti aircraft sights and any company property with the exception of Belt boxes will be returned to camp after relief. Belt boxes will be handed over to relieving company.

HANDING OVER.
O.C. No1. Section is responsible that gun positions and dug outs are handed over in a clean and proper condition and that all instructions are made clear to incoming teams. Receipts for all material handed over to be obtained.

COMPLETION OF RELIEF
On completion of relief No1. Section will return to AUSTRALIA CAMP.

J A Hooper CAPT.
COMDG. 219 COMPANY M.G. CORPS

ISSUED AT 1.30 pm
ACKNOWLEDGE

COPY. No. 1 HQRS
   "   " 2 O.C. No1. Section
   "   " 3 TRANSPORT
   "   " 4 O.C. 96 M.G.C
   "   " 5 WAR DIARY
   "   " 6
   "   " 7 FILE.

SECRET.   Appendix No 9   September 29th 1917.

OPERATION ORDER No 36.
Map Ref. NIEUPORT. Sheet 5/4. 1/10000
EDITION 1

COPY No. 6

RELIEF.
The Subsection of No. 4 Section at present on Anti-Aircraft duty at M.32.a.60.20 and M.32.a.50.10 will be relieved by 3 p.m. on the 30th inst by two Lewis Guns of the 14th Infantry Bde, and on relief will proceed to occupy positions at M.35.c.20.90.

EQUIPMENT.
Guns, Tripods, A.A. Sights, ammunition and all company property will be transferred to new positions. Emplacements and Billets will be handed over in a clean and proper condition and full receipts obtained.

TRANSPORT
One half limber will be at "Three Kings Farm" at 3 p.m. to bring back officers kit and any surplus material.
Five pack animals (two fitted with four panniers) will be at THREE KINGS FARM at 7 p.m. to transport Guns etc to new positions. Eight belt boxes per gun only to be taken, remainder to be returned to H.Q.

RATIONS
Unconsumed portion of days rations to be carried on men. Rations for 1st to be carried on one of mules detailed in para 3.

COMPLETION OF RELIEF.
To be reported by runner to A.H.Q. by word "CHEERS". A.HQ. to report direct to "SOME" quoting reference GS 1368/3/8.

ISSUED AT 1.30 pm
ACKNOWLEDGE

CAPT.
COMDG. 219 COMPANY M.G. CORPS

COPY No 1 HQRS.
" " 2 O.C. No 4 Section
" " 3 A.H.Q
" " 4 T.O.
" " 5 WAR DIARY
" " 6 " "
" " 7 FILE "

CONFIDENTIAL

WAR DIARY.
of
219 MACHINE GUN COY.

Volumn. 8.

From. October. 1st 1917.   To. October. 31st. 1917.

Army Form C. 2118.

WAR DIARY
INTELLIGENCE SUMMARY
(Erase heading not required.)

Instructions regarding War Diaries and Intelligence Summaries are contained in F.S. Regs., Part II. and the Staff Manual respectively. Title pages will be prepared in manuscript.

Place	Date	Hour	Summary of Events and Information	Remarks and references to Appendices
NIEUPORT	October 1st 2nd		Dispositions unchanged. No unusual activity	
"	3rd		Subsection of No 1 Section relieved Subsection of No 3 Section in BRIQUETTERIE and subsection No 1 relieved subsection No 1 at approx M 35 c 2 9 as per O O No 37. Relief completed by 9.30 p.m without undue shelling or incident	Appendix No 1.
"	4/5th		Dispositions unchanged.	
"	6th		No 1 Section relieved by 10th Manchester Regt as per O O No 38. Relief completed by 2 a.m. without casualties.	Appendix No 2.
BRAY DUNES	7th	1.30 pm	Company less one section moved to BRAY DUNES area. Move completed in violent weather by 5 pm and company comfortably settled in billets. See O O No 40	Appendix No 3.
		10.30 pm	No 2 Section relieved in PRESQU'ILE by Section of 1x7 M G Coy as per O.O No 39. Relief completed by 12.30 without incident section returning to COXYDE	" No 4
do	8th		Day spent improving billets, drying clothes etc	
		3 pm	No 2 Section marched in from COXYDE	

Army Form C. 2118.

WAR DIARY

or

INTELLIGENCE SUMMARY.

(Erase heading not required.)

Instructions regarding War Diaries and Intelligence Summaries are contained in F. S. Regs., Part II. and the Staff Manual respectively. Title pages will be prepared in manuscript.

Place	Date	Hour	Summary of Events and Information	Remarks and references to Appendices
BRAY-DUNES	October 9th/13th		Training as per training programme	Vide Appendix No 5
do	14th		Recreational training and rest	Vide
do	15th/20th		Training as per training programme	Vide Appendix No 6
do	21st		Recreational training	Vide
do	22nd/24th		Training as per training programme	Vide Appendix No 7
TETEGHEM	25th	8.0 am	Move to Teteghem area as per O.O. N° 41. Company arrived in billets 11.40 am	Vide Appendix No 8
l'ERKELSBRUGGE area	26th	1.30 am	Move to l'ERKELSBRUGGE area as per O.O No 42. Company billeted in scattered farms in A16.a. area (sheet 27). Weather very stormy. Billets reached 4.30 pm	Vide Appendix No 9
do	27th		Reorganizing billets and drying clothing	Vide
do	28th		Recreational training and rest	Vide
do	29th/31st		Training as per training programme	Vide Appendix No 10

SECRET   Appendix. I.   OCTOBER 2nd

OPERATION ORDER No 347

Map Ref NIEUPORT 12 S.W. 1/20000.

219 M.G Coy.   COPY No 7

RELIEF. An intercompany relief will take place on the night of OCTOBER 3/4th as follows
1. Sub-section of No. 1 section to relieve Sub. section of No 3. section in the BRIQUETTERIE
2. Subsection of No 1 Section to relieve subsection of No 4. section at approx. M.35.c.2.9

PARADE No 1 Section will parade at 5 pm in fighting order. After passing OOST DUNKIRK Section will march in teams at not less than 50ˣ interval.

EQUIPMENT Spare parts only will be exchanged. Guns Tripods ammunition etc will be handed over to relieving teams

HANDING OVER Section officers are responsible that the handing over is carried out correctly in every detail and that all schemes and special features of each emplacement are made clear to incoming teams

TRANSPORT Pack animals required will parade 5 pm

RATIONS. Unconsumed portion of days rations to be carried by the men. Rations for the following day to be carried on Pack animals

COMPLETION OF RELIEF. Completion of relief will be reported to A.HQ. by word "TIRED" by outgoing teams. On completion outgoing sections to proceed to AUSTRALIA CAMP. and to march in Gun teams at intervals of not less than 50ˣ.

ISSUED AT 11 am.
ACKNOWLEDGE

COPY	No 1	HQRS
"	" 2	A.HQ.
"	" 3	O.C No 1 Section
"	" 4	" No 3 "
"	" 5	" No 4 "
"	" 6	TRANSPORT OFFICER
"	" 7	WAR DIARY
"	" 8	" "
"	" 9	FILE

SECRET.   Appendix 2.   October 5th 1917.

219 MGC.   OPERATION ORDER No. 38   COPY 6
         Map Ref. NIEUPORT 12 S.W. 1/20000.

RELIEF.

No.1. Section 219th M.G. Coy. will be relieved in the LOMBARTZYDE Sector of NIEUPORT on the night of the 6/7th October as follows.
a. 2 Guns at M.30.a.20.60 by 2 Lewis guns of the 10th MANCHESTER Regt.
b. 2 Guns at M.35.c.20.90 withdrawn without relief.

HANDING OVER

All defence schemes, information about the line, work in progress, trench stores, water tins, ammunition (S.A.A.) Bombs etc will be handed over on relief. Only such trench maps as contains information which has been added to them will be handed over. Other maps to be retained. Receipts will be obtained in quadruplicate, one copy to be retained by relieving unit, remainder to be sent to Orderly Room without delay.
All Guns, Tripods, belt boxes, periscopes and any other company property other than trench stores will be withdrawn.

TRANSPORT.

5. Pack mules for (a) Relief will be at ration dump at 8.30 pm.
5 Pack mules for (b) Withdrawal will be at ration dump at 7.0 pm.

COMPLETION OF RELIEF.

On completion of relief, teams will return to AUSTRALIA CAMP marching at not less than 50x intervals.
Completion to be reported to A.H.Q. by runner. A.H.Q. to report relief to "SCAN" by code as follows.

```
        RELIEF COMPLETE        SWAT
        MUCH SHELLING          THAT
        LITTLE SHELLING        FLY.
```

This report only to be sent when all four teams have been relieved. After completion of relief A.H.Q. will be closed and personnel rejoin Company at Australia Camp.

                                    JA Hooper CAPT.
                                    COMDG. 219 COMPANY M.G. CORPS

ISSUED AT 9.30 pm.   Copy No.1 HQRS
ACKNOWLEDGE.   " 2 AHQ
                                " 3 O.C. No1 Section
                                " 4 2/Lt. Goldman
                                " 5 Transport Officer
                                " 6/7 War Diary
                                " 8 File
                                " 9 2/Lt Wright

SECRET.   Appendix 3   OCTOBER 5th 1917

OPERATION ORDER No. 39

219. M.G.C   Map Ref. NIEUPORT 12 S.W. 1/20000   COPY No. 5

RELIEF

No. 2 Section 219th M.G. Coy. will be relieved in the PRESQU'ILE by one section of 127th M.G. Coy. on the night of 7/8th October.

HANDING OVER.

All defence schemes information about the line, work in progress, trench stores, water tins, ammunition (S.A.A.) bombs etc. will be handed over on relief. Only such trench maps as contains information which has been added to them will be handed over. Other maps to be retained. Receipts will be obtained in quadruplicate. One copy to be retained by relieving unit, remainder to be sent to Orderly Room without delay.

All Guns, Tripods, Spare Parts, periscopes, clinometers, lanterns for night firing screens, and any other company property, other than trench stores will be withdrawn. Instructions regarding belt boxes and Guides will be issued later.

TRANSPORT

One limber will be at ration dump at 10.45 p.m.

COMPLETION OF RELIEF.

On completion of relief teams will return to AUSTRALIA CAMP. marching at not less than 50x intervals. Completion of relief to be reported by wire from Bde. Office to TRICK by word "CONTENT"

MOVE

No. 2 Section will remain at AUSTRALIA CAMP. during the night 7/8th and on the 8th Oct. will proceed to BRAY DUNES to join the remainder of the company. O.C. No 2 Section is responsible for seeing that strict attention is paid to March discipline and that billets occupied at Australia camp are left in a clean and proper condition. A certificate to the effect to be handed in on arrival at BRAY DUNES.

March to commence not later than 11.30. am Route via. ADINKIRKE and GHYVELDE BRIDGE

Ad. Hooper CAPT.
COMDG. 219 COMPANY M.G. CORPS

ISSUED AT 9.30pm
ACKNOWLEDGE.

COPY No. 1. GHQ
"   " 2. AHQ
"   " 3. O.C. No 2 Section
"   " 4. Transport Officer
"   " 5. War Diary
"   " 6. File.
"   " 7.
"   " 8. Q.M.S.

SECRET   Appendix 4.   October 6th 1917

OPERATION ORDER No 40

219 M.G.C.   Map Ref DUNKERQUE. Sheet 1a 1/100000.   COPY No 7

MOVE
The 219th M.G. Coy less one section will move from AUSTRALIA CAMP to BRAY DUNES area on the 7th October

ROUTE
COXYDE a.22.b.3.6. Turn left, bear right at W.23.c.8.1. ADINKERKE Main road to Port de GHYVELDE turn right to BRAY DUNES.

PARADE
Company will parade at 1.10 pm in "Fighting Order"

TRANSPORT
Transport will be hooked in and formed up on COXYDE - LA PANNE ROAD, facing west by 1.20 pm.

MARCH DISCIPLINE
Sections will march at 50x interval. March discipline must be strictly maintained. No man is allowed to fall out on the line of march without a chit from O.C. Coy. Any man disregarding this order is liable to a Courtmartial - Brakesmen must not hang on the back of limbers and nothing whatsoever is to be put on the watercart.

OFFICERS. CHARGERS.
To be fully equipped and to carry feeds, water buckets, head ropes, picketing ropes and spare shoes. Only regulation bridles to be worn.

BILLETS
Section officers are responsible for leaving billets in a clean condition and will report this to O.C. Coy by 12.30 pm. Officers are individually responsible that their own billets are left scrupulously clean. The C.S.M. will see that latrines are left in a clean condition.

LIMBERS
Will be packed by 11.30 pm with exception of cooking utensils which will be on limbers not later than 12.15 pm.

RATIONS
Unconsumed portion of Days rations to be carried on men

DINNERS
11.30 am

                                     _____ CAPT.
                                     COMDG. 219 COMPANY M.G. CORPS

ISSUED AT   COPY No 1   HQRS
ACKNOWLEDGE   " 2   O.C. No 1. Section
                     " 3   "   No 3
                     " 4   "   No 4
                     " 5   T.O
                     " 6   C.S.M. and Q.M.S
                     " 7/8 WAR DIARY
                     " 9   FILE

TRAINING PROGRAMME.
219th MACHINE GUN COMPANY
WEEK ENDING OCTOBER 13th 1917

DATE	7 - 7.30	8.30 - 9.30	9.45 - 11.30	11.30 - 12.30	2 - 3 pm.	
Oct 9	P.T	ELEMENTARY GUN DRILL	I.A. FIRING BALL AMMUNITION	CLEANING GUNS AND REFILLING BELTS.	SQUARE DRILL WITH ARMS	Special attention to be paid to training of new men in I.A. Belt filling machine to be used and all N.C.O's to be instructed in same.
Oct 10	P.T	BUILDING EMPLACEMENTS		BARRAGE DRILL	Do	Each Section to build a different type of emplacement and each section to continue the other's work.
Oct 11	SQUARE DRILL	P.T	BARRAGE DRILL	CLEANING GUNS AND OVERHAULING BELTS.	Do	
Oct 12	P.T	ELEMENTARY GUN DRILL	I.A. FIRING BALL AMMO IN BOX RESPIRATORS	CLEANING GUNS AND REFILLING BELTS	Do	
Oct 13	P.T.	SQUARE DRILL WITH ARMS.	BARRAGE DRILL	USE OF ANTI-AIRCRAFT SIGHTS	LECTURE ON DISCIPLINE BY S.O. (INCLUDING SENTRIES AND GUARD DUTIES.	

Appendix 5.

TRAINING PROGRAMME
219th MACHINE GUN COMPANY
Week Ending October 20th 1917.

DATE	7am – 7-30	8-30 – 9-30	9-45 – 11-30	11-30 – 12-30	2 – 3 pm
OCTOBER 15th	P.T	SQUARE DRILL WITH ARMS	Practice. MACHINE GUN BARRAGE		CLEANING GUNS AND REFILLING BELTS.
16th	P.T	SQUARE DRILL WITH ARMS	L.A. with ball ammo in box respirators.	Cleaning Guns and filling belts	Lecture by N.C.O.s on Compass and its uses. Lecture to men "FIRE DIRECTION"
17th	P.T	PREPARING FOR BARRAGE	Practice MACHINE GUN BARRAGE		CLEANING GUNS AND REFILLING BELTS.
18th	P.T	SQUARE DRILL WITH ARMS	BUILDING EMPLACEMENTS		Practice in use of compass and map reading for N.C.O.s Lecture to men on Demonstration of methods of Gun Laying.
19th	SQUARE DRILL	PHYSICAL TRAINING	BARRAGE DRILL Embodying use of CLINOMETERS, DIALS AND AIMING SCREENS	OVERHAULING GUNS AND BELTS	RECREATIONAL TRAINING
20th	P.T	SQUARE DRILL WITH ARMS	RIFLE RANGE AND REVOLVER PRACTICES		Practice in use of compass and map reading for N.C.O.s Remainder "Repairs and adjustments".

Appendix 6.

TRAINING PROGRAMME.
219th MACHINE GUN COMPANY.
WEEK ENDING OCTOBER 27th 1917.

DATE	7 - 7-30 a.m.	8.30 - 9.30	9-45 - 11-30	11-30 - 12-30	2 - 3 p.m.
OCTOBER 22	P.T.	ROUTE MARCH IN MARCHING ORDER			FEET INSPECTION.
23	P.T.	SQUARE DRILL WITH ARMS	REPAIRS and ADJUSTMENTS M.G	PRACTISE CARRYING BELT BOXES INTO ACTION.	KIT INSPECTION
24	P.T.	Do.	"DIGGING IN"	N.C.O's use of Compass and MAP READING. REMAINDER use of ANTI AIRCRAFT sights	RECREATIONAL TRAINING.
25	P.T.	Do.	SECTIONS AT SECTION OFFICER'S DISPOSAL FOR GENERAL REVIEW OF WORK	Ball ammunition	I.A. FIRING.
26	P.T.	ROUTE MARCH IN MARCHING ORDER ~~CANCELLED~~			FILLING AND OVERHAULING BELTS
27	P.T.	SQUARE DRILL WITH ARMS	INSPECTION OF GUNS AND SPARE PARTS.	PRACTICE CARRYING BELT BOXES INTO ACTION.	

Appendix 7.

Appendix 6

OCTOBER 24/17   OPERATION ORDER No 41.   COPY No. 1

219 M.G. COY.   MAP REF. Sheet 19 1/40000   **SECRET**

MOVE. The 219th M.G. Coy. will move from BRAY DUNES to TETEGHEM area on the morning of the 25th OCTOBER.

ROUTE. Port de GHYVELDE main Dunkirk road to H.6.b.6.5.

PARADE. Company will parade BY SECTIONS on the main BRAY DUNES – GHYVELDE ROAD facing south by 8 a.m.

TRANSPORT. Transport will be hooked in and formed up on the road (BRAY DUNES – GHYVELDE) facing south by 7.55 a.m.

MARCH DISCIPLINE. March discipline will be strictly maintained. The regulations contained in ADDENDUM No 1 to be rigidly enforced.

OFFICERS CHARGERS. To be fully equipped with feeds, water-buckets, head ropes, picketing ropes and spare shoes. Only regulation bridles to be worn.

BILLETS. S. Os are responsible that BILLETS are left in a clean condition and will report this to the O.C. Coy. by 7.40 a.m. Officers will also see that their own billets are clean. C.S.M. will see that all latrines are properly left.

LIMBERS. Limbers to be packed by 7-20 a.m. LIMBERS TO BE NEATLY PACKED and ALL COVERS TIGHTLY DRAWN AND PROPERLY FASTENED DOWN.

RATIONS. The unconsumed portion of the days rations will be carried by the men.

REVEILLE   5-30 A.M.
BREAKFAST   6-15 A.M.

ISSUED AT 11.30 a.m.

ACKNOWLEDGE

J.A. Cooper
CAPT.
COMDG. 219 COMPANY M.G. CORPS.

COPY No 1. HQRS
" " 2 O.C. No 1 SECTION
" " 3 " 2 "
" " 4 " 3 "
" " 5 " 4 "
" " 6 TRANSPORT OFFICER
" " 7 } WAR DIARY
" " 8 }
" " 9 FILE

Appendix 8

ADDENDUM No 1 TO O.O. No 41

MARCH DISCIPLINE

Particular attention MUST be paid to march discipline. All ranks are especially warned to see that instructions given below are carefully observed.

1. All sections must keep to the right of the road and each section of fours must march by the right and keep closed up.

2. Immediately the signal to halt is given all ranks will fall out on the right of the road and equipment is to be removed within 10 seconds. Transport Drivers will be dismounted within 30 seconds and will loosen girths and look over their animals at once. Drivers will remain with their animals. All spare horses will be halted with their heads turned towards the centre of the road.

3. No man will FALL OUT on the line of march without receiving permission from O.C. Coy. to do so and a chit stating permission has been given.

4. Brakesmen will march clear of vehicles and no article to be placed on the limber covers. No article except the drivers rifle will be placed on the WATER CART. Brakesmen will salute by slinging their rifles and turning head and eyes smartly in the desired direction. THEY WILL NOT SLOPE ARMS. Only one brakesman per vehicle is to be provided except the Mess cart which may have two Brakesmen will march directly behind the limber, and not outside the wheel of the limber.

5. WATER may only be drunk from water bottles after permission has been given by O.C. Coy at least 1 hour AFTER beginning of march. WATER BOTTLES ARE NOT TO BE REFILLED FROM HOUSES OR PUMPS on the line of march.

6. SMOKING is NOT permitted until after the first hour and then only after permission has been given by O.C. Coy.

BREAKDOWN

If a vehicle breaks down, however short the delay is likely to be, it will be got as far as possible off the road, and the column behind will pass it.

When it has been righted it will fall into the column wherever it happens to be, and no effort will be made to regain its right place until a regular halt occurs, and then only if it can be done without blocking the road.

OPERATION ORDER No 42

Appendix 9

SECRET

OCTOBER 25th 1917.
MAP REF. SHEET 19 1/40000

219. M.G. Coy.
COPY No

MOVE.
The 219th M.G. Coy will move from TETEGHEM area on the morning of the 26th inst.

DRESS.
Fighting Order. ALL TIN HELMETS TO BE WORN ON THE LEFT SHOULDER.

PARADE
Company will parade under SECTION ARRANGEMENTS to be on the TETEGHEM ROAD facing east at 7.20 am.

TRANSPORT.
Transport to be formed up at section intervals on road at 7.10 am

LIMBERS. will be packed NOT LATER than 6-35 am.

MARCH DISCIPLINE
The strictest march discipline to be observed. Instructions given in Addendum. No 1 to O.O.41 to be carried out in every detail. NO MAN WILL BE ALLOWED TO DRINK FROM HIS WATER BOTTLE BEFORE 11 am.

OFFICERS CHARGERS to be fully equipped with feeds water buckets, head ropes, picketing ropes and spare shoes. Only regulation bridles to be worn.

BILLETS.
Section officers are responsible that BILLETS are left in a clean and proper condition and will report this to O.C.Coy. by 7.15.

RATIONS.
The unconsumed portion of the days rations to be carried by the man.

G.S. WAGON. will accompany the unit to starting point 1·34·a·6·8 where it will join DIVISIONAL TRAIN.

REVEILLE. 5 am.
BREAKFAST. 5-30 am.

ISSUED AT 4 pm
ACKNOWLEDGE

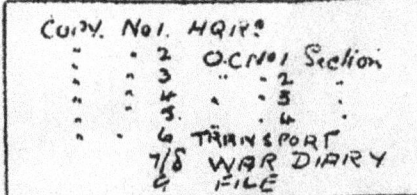

Copy. No 1. HQRs
" " 2 O.C No 1 Section
" " 3 " 2 "
" " 4 " 3 "
" " 5 " 4 "
" " 6 TRANSPORT
" 7/8 WAR DIARY
" 9 FILE

TRAINING PROGRAMME.
219th MACHINE GUN COMPANY.
WEEK ENDING NOVEMBER 3RD 1917

DATE	7am - 7.30	8.30 - 9.30	9.45 - 11.30	11.30 - 12.30	2 - 3 pm.
OCTOBER 29th	P.T.	SQUARE DRILL WITH ARMS	ADVANCED GUN DRILL	CLEANING GUNS AND SPARE PARTS.	KIT INSPECTION.
30th	P.T.	Do.	USE OF GROUND AND COVER.	ONE MAN GUN DRILL	CLEANING GUN AND AMMUNITION
31st	P.T.	Do	"DIGGING IN"	PRACTICE CARRYING AMMO INTO ACTION.	RECREATIONAL TRAINING.
NOVEMBER 1st	P.T.	Do	BARRAGE DRILL	LECTURE ON FIRE DIRECTION.	I.A.
2nd	P.T.	Do	BARRAGE DRILL.	CLEANING GUNS AND AMMUNITION	
3rd	P.T	ROUTE MARCH			FEET INSPECTION

Appendix 10

CONFIDENTIAL

WAR DIARY

OF

219 MACHINE GUN COY.

Volume 9.

From Nov: 1st 1917. To Nov: 30th 1917.

Army Form C. 2118.

WAR DIARY
or
~~INTELLIGENCE SUMMARY~~
(Erase heading not required.)

Instructions regarding War Diaries and Intelligence Summaries are contained in F. S. Regs., Part II. and the Staff Manual respectively. Title pages will be prepared in manuscript.

Place	Date	Hour	Summary of Events and Information	Remarks and references to Appendices
LES WELS BRUGE	Nov. 1st 3rd		Training as per training programme	Appendix No 1
do	4th		Recreational training.	
do	5th to 8th		Training as per training programme	Appendix No 2.
do	9th		Address by G.O.C division.	
do	10th		Route march.	
ARNEKE	11th		Move to ARNEKE area as per O.O. No 43. Arrived in billets at 2.30 p.m.	Appendix No 3
WINNEZEELE	12th		Move to WINNEZEELE area as per O.O No 44. Arrived in billets at 2 p.m.	Appendix No 4.
POPPERINGHE	13th		Move to POPPERINGHE area as per O.O. No 45. Arrived in billets at School Camp (L3 sheet 21) at 12.30 p.m. Company comfortably settled in huts.	Appendix No 5.

WAR DIARY
INTELLIGENCE SUMMARY

Army Form C. 2118.

Place	Date	Hour	Summary of Events and Information	Remarks and references to Appendices
POPPERINGHE	14th		Cleaning up and improvements to camp	fair
do	15th		General training including barrage drill and lectures on direct overhead covering fire. HG·O·R attached from Infantry.	fair
do	16th		General training including "use of ground and cover"	fair
do	17th		Demonstration of use of Yukon pack for machine gun work to machine gun Coy. Commander and Corps Machine gun officer	fair
do	18th		Church Parade and recreational training	fair
do	19th		Training - "Barrage drill"	fair. Appendix No. 6.
do	20th		do "Gas drill and German machine gun. 2/Lt L.W.Brunnagel Transport officer evacuated sick.	fair
do	21st		Training and preparations for move	
IRISH FARM	22nd		Move to IRISH FARM by rain - Transport by road to Brake Camp - Company settled in billets 7 pm	Map Ref Sheet 28 fair Appendix No. 7

Army Form C. 2118.

WAR DIARY

INTELLIGENCE SUMMARY.

(Erase heading not required.)

Instructions regarding War Diaries and Intelligence Summaries are contained in F. S. Regs., Part II. and the Staff Manual respectively. Title pages will be prepared in manuscript.

Place	Date	Hour	Summary of Events and Information	Remarks and references to Appendices
IRISH FARM	23rd		Two sections (No 3 and 4) relieved two sections 216th M.G. Coy on S.O.S. work at YETTA HOUSES D.3.d. 5.8. Relief completed by 10 a.m. without incident.	SPRIET 10000 Appendix No 8
do	24th		Dispositions unchanged. H.Q. moved to CANAL BANK.	fair
CANAL BANK	25th		No. 1 and 2 Sections relieved No. 3 and 4 Sections in line. Relief completed without incident	fair
do	26th		Dispositions unchanged	fair
do	27th		No 3 and 4 Sections relieved No 1 and 2 Sections. Moderate enemy shelling throughout day which increased to heavy bombardment during night	fair
do	28th		Hostile artillery active throughout night. Guns commenced harassing fire on sensitive points behind enemy line. 5000 rounds expended	fair
do	29th		No 1 and 2 Sections relieved No 3 and 4 Sections. Moderate shelling. 1500 rounds fired on sensitive points. Two O.R. killed whilst firing.	fair
do	30th	5 a.m.	5000 rounds fired in response to S.O.S. signal. No 3 and 4 Sections proceeded to line to take up battery positions for an offensive action. No 1 and 2 Sections moved to positions at D.4.a.9.5. All moves completed without incident	fair

Appendix No 1

TRAINING PROGRAMME
219 MACHINE GUN COMPANY.
Week ending NOVEMBER 3RD 1917

DATE	7 - 7.30	8-30 - 9.30	9.45 - 11-30	11-30 - 12-30	2 - 3 pm
MONDAY OCT. 29th	P.T.	Square drill with arms	Advanced Gun drill.	Cleaning guns and Spare parts.	Kit inspection.
TUESDAY OCT. 30th	P.T.	do	Use of Ground and cover.	One man gun drill	Cleaning guns and ammunition.
WEDNESDAY OCT. 31st	P.T.	do	"Digging in"	Practice carrying ammunition into action.	Recreational training
THURSDAY NOV. 1st	P.T.	do	Barrage drill.	Lecture on Fire direction.	V.A.
FRIDAY NOV 2nd	P.T.	do	Barrage drill	Cleaning guns and ammunition	
SATURDAY NOV 3rd	P.T.	ROUTE MARCH			Foot inspection.

Appendix No. 2

TRAINING PROGRAMME
219 MACHINE GUN COMPANY
Week ending November 10th 1917.

DATE	7 – 7-30	8-30 – 9-30	9-45 – 11-30	11-30 – 12-30	2 – 3 pm
November 5th	P.T	Square drill with arms	Practice in use of "YUKON Packs" and carrying ammunition into action.		Practice in use of Compass and marching on compass bearing
6th	P.T	do	Action from Limbers and pack animals.		Cleaning guns and parts
7th	Square drill with arms.	P.T.	9-45 – 11-0. BARRAGE DRILL. 11-0 – 11-45. Tactical employment of M.G's in defence 11-45 – 12-30. CLEANING GUNS and PARTS		
8th		ROUTE MARCH			FEET INSPECTION
9th	P.T	Square drill with arms	9-45 – 11-0 Tactical employment of M.G's IN ATTACK 11-0 – 11-45 DIGGING IN 11-45 – 12-30. Cleaning Guns and parts		
10th	S.D	8-30 – 9-0. P.T.	9-0 – 10-30. BARRAGE DRILL 10-30 – 12-30 Sections at section-officers disposal		Cleaning guns and parts.

[SECRET.]   OPERATION ORDER Nº 43.   Appendix Nº 3

COPY Nº 7   Ref. Sheet 27 - 1/10000   219th M.G.C

MOVE.
The 219th M.G. Coy. will move from ERINGHEM area to ARNEKE area on the morning of the 11th inst.

DRESS.
MARCHING ORDER. all steel helmets to be worn on Packs.

PARADE.
Company will parade under Section Arrangements, to be on the road outside 3 and 4 sections billets facing N.E at 12·10.

TRANSPORT.
Transport to be formed up at section intervals on road at 11·55 am.
Limbers will be packed not later than 10 am.

MARCH DISCIPLINE
The strictest march discipline to be observed. Instructions given in addendum No 1. to O.O. 43 to be carried out in every detail. NO MAN WILL BE ALLOWED TO DRINK FROM HIS WATER-BOTTLE BEFORE 1. pm.

OFFICERS CHARGERS to be fully equipped, with Feeds, water buckets, head ropes, picketing ropes and spare shoes. Only regulation bridles to be worn.

BILLETS.
Section officers are responsible that BILLETS are left in a clean and proper condition and will report to O.C. Coy by 12 noon.

RATIONS.
The unconsumed portion of the days rations to be carried by the man.

DINNER 11 am.

J.F. Allin Lieut.
for CAPT.
COMDG. 219 COMPANY M.G. CORPS

ISSUED AT 11 am.
ACKNOWLEDGE

COPY NO 1. HQRS
" " 2 O.C. No 1 Section
" " 3 " " 2
" " 4 " " 3
" " 5 " " 4
" " 6 TRANSPORT
" " 7/8 WAR DIARY
" " 9 FILE.

Appendix No 4.

OPERATION ORDER No. 44

SECRET.

Map. Ref. Sheet 27. 1/40000.

COPY No _____

219. M.G Coy.

MOVE
The 219th M.G Coy. will move from ARNEKE area to WINNEZEELE area on the morning of the 12th inst.

DRESS.
MARCHING ORDER. Brakemen's packs to be carried on limbers.

PARADE
Company will parade under section arrangements to be on the road outside billets facing N.E at 9.10 am.

TRANSPORT.
To be formed up on road facing N.E at 9 am.
"Special attention to be paid to transport drivers dismounting at the hourly halts. Immediately the whistle is blown twice drivers will prepare to dismount and immediately all the drivers of a section are ready, the section officer will give the signal for them to dismount. This must be done without a moment's loss of time".

LIMBERS
To be packed by 8 am.

MARCH DISCIPLINE
The instructions issued with O.O. No 43 to be strictly carried out.

REVEILLE 6. am.

BREAKFAST. 6.45 am

J.F. Allin Lieut.
for CAPT.
COMDG. 219 COMPANY M.G. CORPS

ISSUED AT 6.10 pm
ACKNOWLEDGE

COPY No 1. - O.C. No 1 Section
2   HQRS.   —
3   —   . 2   —
4   —   . 3   —
5   —   . 4   —
6   TRANSPORT
7/8 WAR DIARY
9   FILE

Appendix No 5 OPERATION ORDER No 45   SECRET.
Map Ref: Sheet 27 1/40000.
COPY No.   219th M G Coy

MOVE

The 219th M.G Coy. will move from the WINNEZEELE area to the POPERINGHE area on the morning of the 13th inst.

DRESS

FIGHTING ORDER. Steel helmets will be worn on back of haversack.

PARADE

Company will parade under Section arrangements, outside HQRS at 8 am.

TRANSPORT

Transport to be formed up on the ONSEZELLE - HEATZELLE ROAD facing N.E. J2.b.99 at 8 am.

LIMBERS to be neatly packed by 7 am.

BLANKETS and SOYER STOVE to be deposited at J3.c.0.3 by 7.20 am. These stores to be in charge of 11201 Cpl. Murray. W
  90930. Pte Taylor N
  91180 Pte Thomas. H.

REVEILLE 5 am.

BREAKFAST 5.45 am.

ISSUED AT
ACKNOWLEDGE

J.F. Allen /Capt.
COMDG. 219 COMPANY M.G. CORPS.

COPY No 1 HQRS
  "   " 2 O.C No 1 Section
  "   " 3 "   " 2   "
  "   " 4 "   " 3   "
  "   " 5 "   " 4   "
  "   " 6 TRANSPORT
  "   " 7 WAR DIARY
  "   " 8
  "   " 9 FILE

Appendix No. 6.

TRAINING PROGRAMME
219th MACHINE GUN COMPANY.
Week ending November 24th 1917

DATE	9am - 9-45	10 a.m. - 11 am.	11 am - 12.30	6 p.m.	ATTACHED MEN
MONDAY NOV 19	SQUARE DRILL	Barrage drill.	Practice with "Yukon pack".		
TUESDAY NOV 20	P.T.	Marching on Compass bearing	Gun drill from limbers.	Laying guns by night	
WEDNESDAY NOV 21	SQUARE DRILL	TACTICAL EXERCISE Machine guns in defence.			Attached men to be instructed in GUNDRILL, MECHANISM, STOPPAGES and to fire gun on range in L.G.C.
THURSDAY NOV. 22	P.T.	Barrage drill in Box respirators.	Lecture on fire direction.	Preparing barrage positions by night	
FRIDAY NOV. 23	SQUARE DRILL	Overhauling and repairing belts	Barrage drill.		
SATURDAY NOV 24.	P.T.	TACTICAL EXERCISE Machine guns in attack.			

SECRET.

219 M.G.Company.

Appendix No. 7
21/11/17

OPERATION ORDER No. 46.
Map ref. Sheet 28.

Move.

The 219th. M.G.Company will move from the POPERINGHE Area to the forward area on the morning of the 22nd. inst., as follows:-

(a) Personnel by train from POPERINGHE to IRISH FARM.

(b) Transport by road to Brake Camp.

Dress.

Full marching order.

Limbers.

Limbers will be packed by 7.30 a.m., and to be on road facing Camp entrance at 9.0 a.m. All limbers to be neatly packed and covers neatly tied down.

March discipline.

Special attention is to be paid to march discipline by transport especially in regard to mounting and dismounting at halts, which will be done by signal from the head of the column.

Rations.

The unconsumed portion of the days rations to be carried by the men.

Reveille 6.0 a.m.
Breakfast 6.30 a.m.
Parade for Sections 8.0 a.m.

Copy No. 1 to HQ.
2 .. No.1 Sect.
3 .. No.2 ....
4 .. No.3 ....
5 .. No.4 ....
6 .. T.O.
7 .. W. Diary
8
9 .. File.

ACKNOWLEDGE.

F.A.Hooper.
CAPT.
COMDG. 219 COMPANY M.G. CORPS.

Secret.

Appendix No 8.

OPERATION ORDER No. 47
Map ref. Sheet no.28

Copy No. 7   219 M.G.Coy.

Relief.

219 M.G.Coy. will relieve 216 M.G.Coy. in the Spriet Sector on the morning of the 23rd. inst. as follows :-
   No. 3 Section on right.
   No. 4 Section on left.

Parade.

Sections will parade at 7.30 a.m., in fighting order, overcoats to be worn. Gas Helmets to be worn in alert position.

Equipment.

Guns and spare parts only will be taken --- ammunition boxes and tripods will be taken over from 216 M.G.Coy.

Rations.

Rations for 48 hours will be taken.

Carriers.

Four men per section will be detailed. One carrier per section will proceed with the relief, afterwards returning to Camp.

Reports.

Tactical reports will be sent to H.Q. 97 Inf. Bde. at Kansas Farm.
All other reports, details of casualties etc. to be sent to Coy. H.Q.

                                            J Attoow
                                                      CAPT.
                                       COMDG. 219 COMPANY M.G. CORPS.

Reveille: 6.0 a.m.   Copy No. 1 H.Q.
Breakfast 6.45 a.m.   2 No.1 Section
                                         3 No.2 ..
                                         4 No.3 ..
                                         5 No.4 ..
Issued at 8.30 p.m.   6 Transport
                                         7
Acknowledge: 8 War diary
                                         9 File.

Vol 10

CONFIDENTIAL

WAR DIARY

OF

219 MACHINE GUN COY.

VOLUME 10.

FROM DECEMBER 1st 1917.   TO DECEMBER 31st 1917.

Army Form C. 2118.

WAR DIARY

INTELLIGENCE SUMMARY

(Erase heading not required.)

Instructions regarding War Diaries and Intelligence Summaries are contained in F. S. Regs., Part II. and the Staff Manual respectively. Title pages will be prepared in manuscript.

Place	Date	Hour	Summary of Events and Information	Remarks and references to Appendices
YPRES CANAL BANK	Dec 1st	6 a.m.	Sixteen guns in barrage positions at D4 a.9.5.	
		5 pm	All guns laid on barrage lines and ready to open fire at laid down in O.O. No 48.	Appendix No I
do	2nd	1.55 am	Infantry advanced to the attack	
		2.3	Barrage opened as laid down in programme, and maintained for two hours. During this period the hostile shelling of the position was not unduly heavy but one direct hit was made on an ammunition dump killing two men and wounding two others	
		6 am	Barrage reopened and continued until 8 am.	
		8.20 am	Concentrated fire was opened on enemy massing near Valuation Houses and maintained for five minutes.	
		9.20 a	Barrage reopened and continued until 9.40 am.	
		12 noon	Barrage reopened and maintained until 12.30 pm to cover a further infantry attack.	
		4.6 pm	The enemy put down a heavy barrage and counter-attacked. S.O.S was sent up to which all guns immediately responded and fired for 20 minutes. During this period a further hit was experienced on a gun emplacement and eight more men were wounded.	

WAR DIARY
INTELLIGENCE SUMMARY

Army Form C. 2118.

Place	Date	Hour	Summary of Events and Information	Remarks and references to Appendices
YPRES	3rd		From 5 P.M. onwards harassing fire was carried out on sensitive points within range	tak
			The infantry attack was not successful being held up by machine gun fire at close range and on several points on the 3rd our line was withdrawn to the original jumping off line.	tak
			Throughout the operation a total of 240,000 rounds were fired, the total casualties experienced being two killed and ten wounded	tak
			No.1552 Sgt. Davies W.S. particularly distinguished himself in tending (wounded) under shell fire for this he was awarded the Military Medal at a later date	tak
do	4th		Harassing fire was continued throughout the whole of the 4th on selected points behind the enemy lines	tak
do	5th		Eight guns were withdrawn to Canal Bank at dusk and remainder resumed their positions at YETTA Houses and continued to carry out harassing fire	tak
do	6th		The teams in the line were replaced by fresh teams from reserves. Whilst coming from the line three men were killed by shell fire on the	tak

WAR DIARY

INTELLIGENCE SUMMARY

Army Form C. 2118.

Place	Date	Hour	Summary of Events and Information	Remarks and references to Appendices
YPRES	6th		duckboard tracks.	talk
	7th to 26th		Throughout this period eight guns were maintained in the line at YETTA HOUSES Position (D20-SPRET 10000) and harassing fire was carried out on sensitive points, a daily average of 8000 rounds being fired. Teams were relieved every 3 days and hot tea supplied to the line daily. On the 10th 2/Lt J W GOLDMAN was admitted to hospital suffering from a sprained knee and evacuated. On the 15th Lt F.A LOTT was transferred to 14th M.G Coy as Second in Command. These officers were replaced by LT J.A. ELDER and 2/Lt W.T LOVETT from the Base.	talk talk talk talk
do	27th		Dispositions unchanged. At 7.50 p.m S.O.S signal was observed on right of Divisional front. All guns opened on their S.O.S lines and continued firing until 8.30 pm – 20000 rounds being expended	talk
do	28th		Dispositions unchanged. Situation normal.	talk

Army Form C. 2118.

WAR DIARY
INTELLIGENCE SUMMARY

(Erase heading not required.)

Place	Date	Hour	Summary of Events and Information	Remarks and references to Appendices
YPRES	29th		Four guns under 2/Lt LOVETT relieved four guns of 96th M.G. Coy at GENOA and VON TIRPITZ FARMS as per O.O. No. 49. Relief completed at 10 a.m. without incident.	Appendix No. 2
do	30th		Dispositions unchanged.	
do	31st	6.15am	S.O.S seen on Divisional Front. Guns at YETTA HOUSES fired 1000 rounds on S.O.S lines.	
		10.30 am	All guns relieved by guns of 228th M.G.Coy as per O.O. No. 5(G). Relief completed by 10.30 a.m. and teams returned to CANAL BANK.	Appendix No. 3

29/11/17   Appendix No 1   Secret.

219 M.G.Coy.

OPERATION ORDER No.48
Map Ref. SPRIET 1/10000

Para. 1.

The 219th. M.G.Company will take part in Offensive Operations and will provide, 2--8 gun batteries to be located at approx. D.4.a.95:-

"K" Battery to be commanded by Lt. F.A.Lott.

"L" Battery to be commanded by 2/Lt. J.W.Goldman.

TARGETS ALLOTTED ARE SHEWN ON MAP ATTACHED.

Para. 2.

RATE OF FIRE as per Appendix "A" attached.

Para. 3.

S.O.S. lines are shewn in RED on map.
Battery Commanders will impress upon all ranks the necessity of recognising quickly and answering promptly all S.O.S. Signals. 6 full belts must always be kept for S.O.S. Should the enemy artillery put down after Zero a barrage similar to that which might be used to cover a counter attack guns will open fire at the rate of 60 rounds per minute as a precautionary measure.

Para. 4. S.O.S. RATE OF FIRE.

One belt in first minute, then 100 rounds per minute for 10 minutes, then 60 rounds per minute until situation is clear.

Para. 5. HEAVY HARASSING FIRE.

Heavy harassing fire will be carried out before and after the attack, except from Zero to 5.30 p.m. on the day after the attack.

Para. 6.

Each gun of the "Barrage Batteries" should have assembled by Zero hour at the gun position,
24000 rounds S.A.A.,   20 filled belts,   1 spare barrel
1 pint of oil.

Para. 7.

Barrage positions will be occupied as follows:-

"K" Battery from positions at YETTA HOUSES to barrage positions to start at 4 p.m. on the 30th.

"L" Battery from Canal Bank starting at 1 p.m. on the 30th.

Para. 8.

"L" Battery, on arriving in positions, will lay on S.O.S. lines of 96 M.G.Company's guns, at present at Yetta Houses.

"K" Battery will move in pairs and on arriving in positions will lay on old OS.O.S. lines. The first pair to move to lay on S.O.S. lines before the second pair moves, and so on.

Para. 9.

In case of enemy attack on XY night or Y day, direct targets will be engaged from the battery positions.

..............................CAPT.
COMDG. 219 COMPANY M.G. CORPS.

ACKNOWLEDGE.

Copy No. 1 to HQ.
        2 to O.C."L"Batt.
        3 to O.C."K" do.
        4 to War Diary
        6 to File.

O.C. 219th. M.G.Company.

SECRET.   30/11/17

Addendum No. 1 to O.O. No. 48

Tracks.

No. 6 Infantry Track is reserved for the 97th. Infantry Brigade from 4 p.m. on the 1st. to 6 a.m. on the 2nd. Dec. No carrying parties will make use of No. 6 Track during this period and anyone on the Track must give way to the 97th. Infantry Brigade.

Report.

At the conclusion of the Operation, Battery Commanders will report number of rounds fired and the action of their guns.

Anti-Aircraft.

One gun of "L" Battery will be detailed to engage hostile aircraft which may come within range.

S.O.S.

S.O.S. Signal will be repeated from Battalion Headquarters at Pillbox 83.

Battery commanders will report when Batteries are ready for action to Group Headquarters near Pillbox 83.

Synchronisation of Watches.

Watches will be synchronised at Group Headquarters at 6.30 p.m

Runners.

One man per Battery will be detailed to act as runner to Group Headquarters.

O.C. 219 M.G.Coy.

Appendix "A" MACHINE GUNS.

BATTERY	TIMES	TASK	RATE OF FIRE etc.
"K" and "L"	(A) Zero plus 8 minutes to Zero plus 2 hours (B) 6 am. to 8 am. (C) 3.30 pm to 5.30 pm (D) On S.O.S. signal	(a), (b), (c) — Open fire on S.O.S. line. One gun of each Sub-section will remain on this line, the other will search continuously between the S.O.S. line and extreme range paying particular attention to the vicinity of dug-outs occupied shell holes, tracks etc. (d) FIRE ON S.O.S. LINE.	(a) During the three Barrage periods 50 Rounds per gun per minute (b) On S O S signal 1. belt in first minutes, then 100 rounds per minute for 10 minutes, then 60 rounds per minute till situation clears.

FIRE ORGANISATION ORDERS.

Composition.	EIGHT GUNS		Battery.		Place.			S.37.
Commanded by	LT J.W.GOLDMAN			Frontage of Battery	70 Y		Date. 20/11/17	Task.
Location of directing gun.	D.4.a.9.55			Grid bearing to R.O.				
No. of Directing gun.	16			Zero line from		through	216	
				Grid bearing of Zero Line.				

No. of Barrage.	No. of Gun.	Targets.	Clock time.	Zero time.	Deviation from Zero line.	Distribution angle.	Range.	V.I.	Q.E.	Range to F.T. when barrage lifts.	Clearance when barrage lifts.	Rate of Fire.
A.	16				0	5°R	2150 x	5M.	5°25'			
B.	15								5°14'			AS PER ORDERS
C.	14	AS PER MAP					60		5°29'			
"	13								5°38'			
"	12						2300 x		5°41'			1700 57"
"	11								5°50'			
"	10								5°59'			
"	9								6°9'			

	8	7	6	5	4	3	2	1	Remarks.
A.	0	43'	1°26'	2°9'	2°50'	3°35'	4°18'	5°	This shows angle from zero line for each gun. From this line barrage chart for each gun is compiled and issued to Gun Commanders.
B.									GUNS NOS. 9-13 SEARCH UP 3°
C.									GUNS NOS 14-16 SEARCH UP 2°

FIRE ORGANISATION ORDERS.

Battery. K. **Place.**   **S.37.**

Date. 29.11.17   **Task.**

Composition.	EIGHT GUNS
Commanded by	LT. F. ALLOTT
Location of directing gun.	D.a.9.55
No. of Directing gun.	8
Frontage of Battery.	70˟
Grid bearing to R.O.	
Zero line from _____ through _____	AS SPECIAL ORDERS
Grid bearing of Zero Line.	29°

No. of Barrage.	No. of Gun.	Targets.	Clock time.	Zero time.	Deviation from Zero line.	Distribution angle.	Range.	V.I.	Q.E.	Range to F.T. when barrage lifts.	Clearance when barrage lifts.	Rate of Fire.
A.	8				0	4°R	2300˟	10 m/m	6°10'	1650˟		AS PER ORDERS ATTACHED
B.	7	AS PER MAP							6°16'			
C.	6						60.		6°22'			
	5								6°28'		104˟	
	4						2400˟		6°34'			
	3								6°40'			
	2								6°46'			
	1								6°52'			

	8	7	6	5	4	3	2	1	Remarks.
A.	0	35'	1°10'	1°45'	2°20'	2°55'	3°30'	4°5'	GUNS Nos. 1 & 5 SEARCH UP 2°
B.									
C.									GUNS Nos. 4 to 8 SEARCH UP 3°

This shows angle from Zero line for each gun. From this line barrage chart for each gun is compiled and issued to Gun Commanders.

219 Machine Gun Company.   **Appendix No 2.**   SECRET

December 27th. 1917.   Copy No. 5

Operation Order No. 49.

Map reference POELCAPPELLE 1/10000

Relief.

    4 guns of 219 M.G.Coy., under 2/Lt. W.J.Lovett, will relieve 4 guns of 96 M.G.Coy. at GENOA and VON TIRPITZ on 29th. December 1917.

Dress.

    Fighting order.

Parade.

    Gun teams of three men per gun will parade at 7.0 a.m. and will proceed by limber to ST. JULIAN.

Guides.

    One guide per gun team will be found by 96 M.G.Coy, and will meet the incoming teams on the plank road by GENOA

Equipment.

    Tripods, belt boxes, A.A. Mountings and Sights will be taken over from 96 M.G.Coy. 4 guns and 4 complete sets of spare parts will be handed to 96 M.G.Coy. on the 28th. inst., and they will transport them to the line and hand them over on relief.

    96 M.G.Coy. will detail one O.R. to remain behind at each position until incoming teams are fully acquainted with lines of fire and orders. These men will be released as soon as the Section Officer is satisfied that gun team Commanders have all information necessary.

Rations.

    Rations for 29th. and 30th., and Breakfast ration for the 31st will be carried by each man.

Handing over.

    Receipts will be given for all equipment taken over. One copy to be returned to Company Headquarters immediately

Completion of Relief.

    Completion of relief will be reported to Company Headquarters by the code word "PRESS"

Runners.

    Two runners to be taken for this purpose, and to act as guides etc.

ACKNOWLEDGE

                                      Copy No. 1 H.Q.
                                         " " 2 2/Lt.Lovett
                                         " " 3 Transport
                                         " " 4 96 M.G.Coy.
                                         " " 5 War Diary
                                         " " 6
                                         " " 7 File

_____ CAPT.
COMDG. 219 COMPANY M.G. CORPS.

Appendix. No 3

219 Company M.G. Corps.   SECRET

December 22nd, 1917.   Copy No. 6

Operation Order No. 51

Map, reference SHEET 1/10000

RELIEF.

The present line of 219 Company, M.G.C. is as follows:-

    2 at ITETA DUMPS.
    2 at SAINT PIERRE.
    2 at BOIS VERTIN FARM.

Will be relieved by the evening of December 23rd 1917 by guns of 224 Co. M.G.C.

MATERIAL.

Tripods, belt boxes, all anti-aircraft sights and mountings, and spares will be handed over to relieving unit; detailed receipt being obtained by each Section Officer; one copy to be retained by relieving unit and one copy handed into Company Headquarters. Guns, condensers bags, spare, and ammunition will not be handed over and will be brought back to Company Headquarters.

HANDING OVER.

Section Officers are responsible for handing over all orders, maps, sketches, and full information in regard to positions and their lines of fire, and will see that these are fully understood by incoming Sections.
The Officer of 224 Co. will point out the position of the reserve emplacements in the Corps line to the Officer who relieves him. Guns from Battery positions will not be moved to these positions until the details have been made known to the relieving units.

GUIDES.

Guides will be provided from each platoon at ITETA DUMPS and at SAINT PIERRE.
Guides to BOIS VERTIN FARM will be found at CROSS ROAD to be provided from Battery.

LIMBERS.

Three limbers will be at RAILHEAD STATION for ITETA DUMPS at 10.15 a.m.
Two limbers will be at CROSS ROAD at 9.30 a.m.

                                                Copy No. 1 H.Q.
                                                        2 BATTERY LINES
                                                        3 RESERVE.
                                                        4 TRANSPORT
                                                        5 WAR DIARY.
                                                        6 FILES.
                                                        8 228 Co.

[signed] CAPT.
COMDG. 219 COMPANY M.G. CORPS

WAR DIARY or INTELLIGENCE SUMMARY

Army Form C. 2118.

17th (S) Batt. Yorkd Fuss. (NE Railway Pioneers)

SHEET No. 32.

Place	Date	Hour	Summary of Events and Information	Remarks and references to Appendices
PESELHOEK	2/9/17		Battalion moved from "P" Camp. A.150.w to by Buses to GHYVELDE. Battalion located at Corps Reinforcement Camp at GHYVELDE.	Gestil Batt.
GHYVELDE	4/9/17		"C" Coy moved to BRISBANE-CAMP to take over work from 9th Seaforth Hdrs.	Gestil Batt.
"	7/9/17		Inspection of Batt. by G.O.C. 32nd Division.	Gestil
OOST DUNKERKE	8/9/17		"A" "B" & "D" Coys marched from GHYVELDE to BRISBANE CAMP. arrived 1.45pm Temporary accommodation and under C.R.E. 32nd Division at NIEUPORT defences.	Gestil
"	9/9/17		Lieut J POTTS reported for duty 15/9 posted to "D" Company	Gestil
"	15/9/17		Lieut A.E. PHELAN and 150 new reinforcements joined Batt. & C Company R.E.	Gestil
"	15/9/17		Lieuts J Dawson – J.W. Gregory – A.K. Wadsworth and 2nd Lieut W. Cameron	Gestil
"	17/9/17		G. McKay – W.D. Maughan joined Batt. for duty	
"	18/9/17		Lieuts F.T. Bacey – G.S. Tindall – B. Gaffney – E.R. Dickinson - 2nd Lt C.B. Mirrilees – W.E. Calvert – W.E. Norris – J.G. Pickburn and 18 O.R. joined	Gestil Batt.
"	22/9/17		Lieut A.E. PHELAN posted to 1st Batt. North'd Fus'rs	Gestil
"	23/9/17		Lieut R. de P Dallin attached to 219th Coy R.E. for duty from 23rd Sept 17	Gestil
"	24/9/17		2nd Lieut Ratcliffe & Piper joined Batt. for duty.	Gestil
"	27/9/17		Draft of 150 O.Ranks transferred to 6th Batt. North'd Fuseliers.	Gestil
"	30/9/17		2nd Lieut Gregory proceed to join 16 K.N.I.F Ankhy Loc. 32nd Division 7 O.R. Wounded & Wounded at duty during month	Gestil

Geofdardin Captain
for O.C. 17th N.F.

Headquarters,
32nd Division.

CONFIDENTIAL.

Herewith War Diary of this Unit for the month of OCTOBER 1917.

Please acknowledge receipt.

[signature] Capt.

Lieut: Colonel,
Commanding, 17th Bn. Northumberland Fusiliers
(NER Pioneers)

October 31st 1917.

WAR DIARY
or
INTELLIGENCE SUMMARY 17TH (S) BATT. NORTHUMBERLAND FUSILIERS.
(NER. PIONEERS)
SHEET No 33

Army Form C. 2118.

Place	Date	Hour	Summary of Events and Information	Remarks and references to Appendices
OOST DUNKERKE.	1/X/17		BATTN. LOCATED AT BRISBANE CAMP. X3. B6. 8. In Billets.	Genl.
—DO—	4/X/17		LIEUT. F. DAWSON PROCEEDED TO JOIN. 16TH N.F. FOR DUTY.	Genl.
—DO—	7/X/17		BATT. MOVE BY MARCH ROUTE FROM BRISBANE CAMP to ADINKIRKE and Barge to H5.D3.6 March Route to COUDEKERQUE.	Genl.
COUDEKERQUE	21/X/17		BATT. MARCHED FROM COUDEKERQUE TO ZERMEZEELE.	Genl.
	23/X/17		MARCH ROUTE FROM ZERMEZEELE TO ARNEKE ENTRAINED FOR BRELAN March out to ST JEAN. BATT ATTACHED TO VIII CORPS FOR DUTY.	Genl.
	20/X/17		LIEUT MITCHELL TO EGYPTIAN ARMY	Genl.
			CASUALTIES DURING MONTH 8 KILLED - 190 OR WOUNDED. 1 OFFR WOUNDED.	Genl.

GW Hardie Capt
Adjt 17th N.F. for O.C.

Army Form C. 2118.

WAR DIARY
or
INTELLIGENCE SUMMARY — 17TH (S) BATT NORTHUMBERLAND FRS (NERPIONEERS)
SHEET No. 34.
(Erase heading not required.)

Vol 24

Place	Date	Hour	Summary of Events and Information	Remarks and references to Appendices
ST JEAN	1/XI/17		Battalion working under orders of C.E. XVIII Corps on Roads from STEENBECK - ST JULIEN - LANGMARCK.	GeoW
	15/XI/17		Battalion transferred from 32ND DIVISION to Railway Construction Troops to be reorganized and equipped as such.	GeoW
	20/XI/17		Lt. W.W. ROBERTSON to DET BASE CALAIS for duty as storekeeper.	GeoW
			2ND Lieut W.D. MAUGHAN KILLED 19.11.17	GeoW
	20/XI/17		Lt Col. W.D.V.O. KING proceeded on Leave. A/MAJOR G.S. TAYLOR assumes Command	GeoW
			100 O.Ranks ex RE rejoined to RE Base	GeoW
	18/17			GeoW
			Casualties during the month:—	GeoW
			Killed 1 Officer and 22 O.R.	
			Wounded 3 Officers and 50 O.R.	

GS Hardie Capt & Adjt
for OC 17th North'd Fus'rs
(NE RAILWAY PIONEERS)

CONFIDENTIAL.

WAR DIARY
OF
219TH COY: MACHINE GUN CORPS.

VOLUME II.

FROM JANUARY 1ST 1918.
TO JANUARY 31ST 1918.

WAR DIARY or INTELLIGENCE SUMMARY.

Army Form C. 2118.

Instructions regarding War Diaries and Intelligence Summaries are contained in F. S. Regs., Part II. and the Staff Manual respectively. Title pages will be prepared in manuscript.

(Erase heading not required.)

Place	Date	Hour	Summary of Events and Information	Remarks and references to Appendices
CANAL BANK	JAN 1st		Move to New Area Delayed	J.7.a. Appendix No 1
	2nd			
do	3rd		Company and Transport Moved to new Area.	J.7.a. do.
GRASSE PAYELLE	4th		Company settled in Billets GRASSE PAYELLE at 3pm.	J.7.a.
do	5th		Cleaning up and improving Billets.	J.7.a.
do	6th		Church Parade and Recreational Training	J.7.a.
do	7th		XMAS HOLIDAY	J.7.a.
do	8th			
do	11th		Training as per Training Programme	J.7.a Appendix No 2
	12th			
do	13th		Church Parade and Recreational Training	J.7.a
do	14th		Training as per Training Programme	J.7.a Appendix No 3.
	15th			
	17th			
do	18th		Preparing for Move	J.7.a.

WAR DIARY
INTELLIGENCE SUMMARY
(Erase heading not required.)

Army Form C. 2118.

Place	Date	Hour	Summary of Events and Information	Remarks and references to Appendices
GRASSE PAYELLE	JAN. 19th		Transport Moved to LANGEMARK Area	J.T.A. Appendix No 4
do	20th		Company Moved to LANGEMARK Area. Company settled in Camp G 1.30/pm.	J.T.A.
LANGEMARK AREA	21st			J.T.A
do	22nd		Cleaning up and improving Billets	J.T.A.
do	23rd		Training. Barrage Drill	J.T.A.
do	24th		Packing and preparing for Move	J.T.A.
do	25th		Company Moved to ELVERDINGHE Area.	J.T.A. Appendix No 5
ELVERDINGHE AREA	26th		Cleaning and improving billets	J.T.A
do	27th		Preparing Guns and equipment for the Line	J.T.A.
do	28th		No 3 Section, with 8 Guns, relieved 53rd M.G. Coy on Right Divisional Front at U.17.c.60.20, U.17.b.40.20, U.16.a.20.25, U.16.a.10.35, U.15.d.20.70, U.15.d.35.60, U.15.Central, U.15.C.10.0p. Relief complete by 2/pm. without incident.	131st SCHOOTE SHEET 20 SW.4 Appendix No 6 J.T.A.

Army Form C. 2118.

WAR DIARY
or
INTELLIGENCE SUMMARY

(Erase heading not required.)

Place	Date	Hour	Summary of Events and Information	Remarks and references to Appendices
ELVER-DINGHE AREA	JAN 28		No 4 Section with 8 Guns, relieved 216th M.G. Coy. on Left Divisional Front. at: U10.c.00.00. U9.d.90.00. U9c.58.25. U9c.30.75. U8d.86.54. U8d.70.58. U8a.55.55. U7.b.90.55. Relief complete by 2/pm without incident.	Appendix No 6. J.F.A. J.F.A.
do	29th		Dispositions Unchanged. Slight hostile shelling at U8d.86.54., stopped by our Artillery.	J.F.A.
do	30th			
do	31st		Dispositions Unchanged.	J.F.A.

Appendix No. 1.

219 Machine Gun Company.   SECRET

Amendment No. 2 to Operatioe Order No. 50

1. The move of 219 Machine Gun Company's Transport will be delayed until further orders.

   The transport of 14 Machine Gun Coy. will not move with that of 219 Machine Gun Coy., but will move under orders to be issued by its own Company.

31/12/17

[signature] CAPT.
COMDG. 219 COMPANY M.G. CORPS.

219 Machine Gun Company   SECRET

Addendum No. 1 to Operation Order No.50

1. Arrival of transport of 219th. Machine Gun Company and 14th. Machine Gun Company at TUNNELLING CAMP and LEDERZEELE will be reported direct to Divisional Headquarters by wire.

30/12/17

                                                                    .... CAPT.
                                                        COMDG. 219 COMPANY M.G. CORPS.

219 Machine Gun Company.   SECRET.

December 29th. 1917.   Copy No. 6

Operation Order No. 50.

Map Reference Sheet 28 1/40000
     "   "   "   5c 1/10000 (Hazebrouck)

1. MOVE.

1. The combined transports of 219 M. and 14th M.G.Companies will move from the forward area to the new area, the move commencing on the 1st. January. 1918.

2. Stages.

The Stages will be as follows:-

    <u>1st. January.</u> From Forward Area to TUNNELLING CAMP.
                  (Route via POPERINGHE, E.SWITCH ROAD)

    <u>2nd. January.</u> From TUNNELLING CAMP to LEDERZEELE Area.
                  (Route via HOUTKERQUE, HERZEELE, WORMHOUT,
                    ZEGGARS CAPELLE)

    <u>3rd. January.</u> From LEDERZEELE Area to New Area.
                  (Route via ST.MOMELIN, WATTEN, BLEUE MAISON,
                   BOYEVAL, NORDAUSQUES)

Transport will be met by guides from their respective Units at NORDAUSQUES at 1.0 p.m. on January 3rd., and will be guided to Units.

3. Billets.

Billets will be obtained for the 1st., from Area Commandant at ST.JAN TER BIEZEN, and on the 2nd. from Area Commandant at LEDERZEELE. 2/Lt. E.G.Lord, 219 M.G.Coy., will act as Billeting Officer for the combined transport.

4. Rations.

Rations and fodder for the 1st. and 2nd. will be carried. Rations for the 3rd. will be delivered to Transport at LEDERZEELE on the evening of the 2nd. by the Supply Column.

5. Discipline.

March Discipline as detailed in Appendix A will be strictly enforced.

6. FORMING UP.

The transport of 219 M.G.Coy. will be formed up on the road at D.30.c.7.5., and will be joined there by the transport of 14.M.G.Coy., at 11.0 a.m. on the morning of the 1st. January. For the remaining days the move will commence not later than 8.0 a.m. daily.

7. Command.

The combined transport will move under the command of 2/Lt. F.Q.Broom, 219 M.G.Coy.

ACKNOWLEDGE.   Copy No.1 14 M.G.Coy.
                                                     2   do. Trans.
                                                     3 Transport
                                                     4 H.Q.
                                                     5
                                                     6 War Diary
          _____ CAPT.   7 FILE
     COMDG. 219 COMPANY M.G. CORPS.

Appendix A.

Transport March Discipline.

1. Turnout.

Special attention will be paid to turn out of animals, harness, and limbers throughout the move. Animals must be properly groomed and harness and limbers clean whatever the conditions may be.
Special attention will be paid to the neat packing of limbers, and that limber covers are stretched tight and securely fastened. Head collar chains must be kept bright and oiled.

2. Halts.

A halt of 10 minutes per hour will be given. Immediately the signal is given, drivers will dismount together, and will loosen girths and look over the animals at once. Drivers will not leave their animals.
All spare horses will be halted with their heads turned towards the centre of the road.

3. Brakesmen.

Brakesmen will march clear of vehicles and no article will be placed on the limber covers. No article except the driver's rifle will be placed on the WATERCART. Brakesmen will salute by slinging their rifles and turning head and eyes smartly in the desired direction. THEY WILL NOT SLOPE ARMS.
Only one brakesman per vehicle is to be provided, except the MESSCART which may have two.
Brakesmen will march directly behind the limber, and not outside the hub of the wheel.

4. Breakdowns.

If a vehicle breaks down, however short the delay is likely to be, it will be got as far as possible off the road, and the column behind will pass it.
When it has been righted, it will fall into the column wherever it happens to be, and no effort will be made to regain its right place until a regular halt occurs, and then only if it can be done without blocking the road.

5. Intervals.

Gaps of 25 yards must be left between each section of six vehicles.

6. Roads.

Transport will not be allowed to halt on the following sections of roads:-
   (a) Roads in BAILLEUL.
   (b) BAILLEUL-LOCRE-SCHERPENBERG-LA CLYTTE-DICKEBUSCH-CAFE BELGE HOUT-VLAMERTINGHE (Halting places have been made off the road at O.3.c; CANADA CORNER (H.17.c central); HALLEBAST).
   (c) Roads through POPERINGHE and YPRES.
   (d) Main VLAMERTINGHE-YPRES and between GOLDFISH CHATEAU and YPRES RAMPART.
   (e) POPERINGHE-Watou road.

(f) BRIELEN-C.25.a.3.8-ZOUAVE VILLA (C.20.c.6.2) road.
(g) Between E.21.a.9.7 and E.16.b.8.2 on road connecting the HOUTKERQUE-WATOU Road with the main WATOU-ROUSBRUGGE Road.

219 Machine Gun Company.   SECRET

Amendment No. 2 to Operation Order No. 52

1. Move as detailed will take place on 2nd. instead of 1st.

2. The following will travel with the lorry:-

   Company Quartermaster Sergeant.
   Orderly Room Clerk.
   1 Company Cook.
   1 Officers' Mess Cook.

                                                        CAPT:
                                        COMDG. 219 COMPANY M.G. CORPS.

219 Machine Gun Company   SECRET

Amendment No. 11 to Operation Order No. 52

1. Move will be delayed until further orders.

                                                        CAPT.
                        COMDG. 219 COMPANY M.G. CORPS.

To. O.C.
   219 M.G.Coy.
      (Through O. i/c M.G.Corps Section
      G.H.Q.)

1. Move will be delayed until further orders.

Amendment No. 1 to Operation Order No. 52

---   ---
1/2/18   219 Machine Gun Company.

219 Machine Gun Company.   SECRET

30/12/17   Copy No. 6

Operation Order No. 52

1. Move.

219th. Machine Gun Company, less Transport, will move from
present Area to New Area on the morning of January 1st 1918.

2. Trains.

Personnel will proceed by train as follows:-
    One Train at PLATEAU SIDING at 6.0 a.m. for XX POPERINGHE.
    One Train from POPERINGHE at 9.0 a.m. to New Area.

3. Parade.

Company will parade at 5.25 a.m. Dress, Full Marching Order.
Overcoats may be worn. Steel Helmets will be worn as far as
POPERINGHE.

4. Lorry.

A portion of a lorry will be available, and will be loaded with
the following :-
    2 blankets per each Officers' Kits,
    9 sizes,   Officers' Mess Basket,
    1 Orderly Room Box and Typewriter.

These stores will be dumped in store tent by not later than
4.45 a.m. All stores other than these must be returned to
Transport Lines by Platoons leaving camp at 11.0 a.m. 31st.

5. Rations.

Rations for the 1st. will be issued on the 31st. and will be
carried individually by the men. Rations for 2nd. will be made
up into man tents and issued at POPERINGHE on the morning of 1st.
All Waterbottles must be filled.

6. Train Discipline.

Train discipline will be strictly enforced. Entraining and
detraining will be carried out in silence. One N.C.O. to be in
charge of each carriage, and will be responsible that no damage
is done and that the carriage is left in a clean and proper
condition. One N.C.O. and three men to be responsible for seeing
that all carriage doors are closed before the train starts.
No man is allowed to leave the train without permission from
O.C. Train. All equipment to be donned 15 minutes before
reaching detraining station.

7. Reveille: 4.0 a.m.   O.C. No.1 O.C. No.1 Sect.
   Breakfasts 4.30 a.m.   "   2   "   No.2 "
   Parade 5.25 a.m.   "   3   "   No.3 "
                                               "   4   "   No.4 "
8. Billets.
Billets will be left clean, and a report to this effect will be
sent to O.C. Company at 9.0 a.m.
                                             Copy No. 1   O.C. No.1 Sect.
                                               "   " 2   "   2   "
                                               "   " 3   "   3   "
                                               "   " 4   "   4   "
                                               "   " 5   G.O.C.
                                               "   " 7   War Diary
                                               "   " 8   Spare.

FCHooper CAPT.
COMDG. 219 COMPANY M.G. CORPS

Appendix No 2.

TRAINING PROGRAMME.
219 MACHINE GUN COMPANY
Week ending JANUARY 12th 1918.

DATE	HOUR	NATURE OF TRAINING	LOCATION
JAN. 7th		XMAS HOLIDAY – – – – – – – –	
JAN. 8th	9 - 9.45	Square drill with arms	Range shooting at 'B' RANGE at "M" in NORTLEULINGHEM
	10 - 12.30	Overhauling and resorting guns and equipment.	
	2 pm	Recreational Training	Other parades in vicinity of billets in GRASSE PAYELLE
JAN. 9th	9 - 12.30	BATTERY No 1. Range shooting for classification of Machine Gunners.	
		BATTERY No 2	
	9 - 9.45	Square drill with arms	
	10 - 11.0	Gun drill	
	11 - 12.30	Lecture on Fire Direction	
	2 pm	Recreational Training	
JAN. 10th	9 - 12.30	BATTERY No 2. Range shooting for classification of Machine Gunners	
		BATTERY No 1	
	9 - 9.45	Square drill with arms	
	10 - 11.0	Gun drill	
	11 - 12.30	Lecture on fire Direction	
	2 pm	Recreational Training	
JAN. 11th	9 - 12.30	BATTERY No 1 Range shooting STOPPAGES	
		BATTERY No 2	
	9 - 9.45	Square drill with arms	
	10 - 11.30	Barrage drill	
	11.30 - 12.30	Cleaning guns and parts	
	2 pm	Recreational Training	
JAN. 12th	9 - 12.30	BATTERY No 2. Range shooting STOPPAGES	
		BATTERY No 1	
	9 - 9.45	Square drill with arms	
	10 - 11.30	Barrage drill	
	11.30 - 12.30	Cleaning guns and parts	
	2 pm	Recreational Training	

Appendix No 3

TRAINING PROGRAMME.
219 MACHINE GUN COMPANY.
Week ending. JANUARY 19th. 1918

DATE	HOUR	NATURE OF TRAINING.	LOCATION
JAN 14	9 am - 9.45 10 - 11.15 11.30 - 12.30 2 pm - 2.30	SQUARE DRILL COMBINED GUN DRILL CLEANING GUNS LECTURE "FIRE DIRECTION"	"GRASSE PAYELLE"
JAN 15	9 am - 9.45 10 - 11.15 11 - 12.30 2 pm - 2.30	SQUARE DRILL T.O.E.T. LECTURE "BARRAGE" CLEANING GUNS	
JAN 16	9 am - 9.45 10 - 11.15 11.30 - 12.30 2 pm - 2.30	SQUARE DRILL "GAS DRILL" ELEMENTARY BARRAGE DRILL PROLONGED STOPPAGES CLEANING GUNS	IN VICINITY OF BILLETS
JAN 17	9 am - 9.45 10 - 11.15 11.30 - 12.30 2 pm - 2.30	P.T LECTURE "M.G's IN DEFENCE". ELEMENTARY SCHEME CLEANING GUNS	
JAN 18	9 am - 9.45 10 - 11.30 11.30 - 12.30 2 pm - 2.30	SQUARE DRILL BARRAGE DRILL "SCHEME" GROUND AND COVER CLEANING GUNS	
JAN 19	9 am - 9.45 10 - 12.30 2 pm - 2.30	SQUARE DRILL "ACTION" FROM LIMBERS AND SCHEME WITH RANGE FINDERS CLEANING GUNS	

Training Programme — N.C.O's

219 Machine Gun Company.

Week ending JANUARY 19th 1918

DATE	NATURE OF TRAINING
JAN 14th	Scope of course and elementary fire direction
JAN 15th	LECTURE --- Fetching and Setting up guns Practical instruction
JAN 16th	LECTURE -- Direct and indirect fire Practical Indirect overhead fire Ground Reconnaissance
JAN 17th	Searching and Traverse slopes. Lecture and practice Indirect shooting Map problems
JAN 18th	Barrages - Lecture and practice
JAN 19th	Barrage Reconnaissance of a defensive position

NOTES IN ADDITION. The following will be practised - Fighting for and selection of gun positions. Organisation of defence.

TRAINING PROGRAMME. ATTACHED MEN.

219 MACHINE GUN COMPANY.

Week ending. JANUARY 19th 1918.

DATE.	9 – 10 a.m.	10 – 11·15 a.m.	11·30 – 12·30	2 – 2·30 p.m.
MONDAY 14	SQUAD DRILL	GUN DRILL	STOPPAGES and CLEANING	LECTURE NECESSARY QUALITIES OF A MACHINE GUNNER
TUESDAY 15	9am – 9·30 P.T	9·45 – 10·45 a.m. STOPPAGES	11 am – 12·30 GUN DRILL	STRIPPING AND CLEANING.
WEDNESDAY 16	SQUAD DRILL	GUN DRILL	STOPPAGES & C. & C.	LECTURE CHARACTERISTICS
THURSDAY 17	Do	STRIPPING PARTS B.D.A.	GUN DRILL & C. & C.	LECTURE DUTIES OF M.G. NUMBERS
FRIDAY 18	9am – 9·30 P.T	10am – 11·15. T.O.E.T	STOPPAGES	LECTURE. M.G. SIGNALS.
SATURDAY 19	FIRING PART 1			

Appendix No 4.

219 Machine Gun Company   SECRET

January 17th. 1919

Operation Order No. 53

Map Reference Sheet 27a N.E. 1/20000
"   "   "   28   1/40000
"   "   "   Hazebrouck 5a 1/100000

1. Move.

The transport of 219 M.G.Coy. (less 2 limbers and watercart) will move to the forward area, move commencing January 19th. 1919.

2. Stages.

The stages will be as follows:-
19th. January. From GRASON PAYELLE area to RUBROUCK area. Starting point, road junction J28a.2.0 NORDAUSQUES. Transport to pass the starting point at 9.39 a.m.
20th. January. From RUBROUCK area to ST JAN TER BIEZEN area. Route via WORMHOUT, HOUTKERQUE.
21st. January. ST JAN TER BIEZEN area to destination. Route via POPERINGHE, H.SWITCH ROAD and CROSS ROADS O3a.2.9

Orders for 20th. and 21st. will be issued by O.C. No.4 Coy. Divisional Train.

3. Billets.

Billets will be obtained on the 19th. from Area Commandant, RUBROUCK, and on the 20th. from Area Commandant ST JAN TER BIEZEN.
2/Lt. R.J.Lovett will act as billeting Officer for the transport.

4. Rations.

Rations for the 19th. will be carried by the men, and for 20th. and 21st. by first line transport.

5. March Discipline.

March discipline as detailed in Appendix A. to be strictly adhered to.

6. Command.

The combined transport of the Brigade will move under the command of O.C. No.4 Coy. Divisional Train.

Issued at.

Acknowledge.   Copy No.1   H.Q.
                                                      2   Transport Officer
                                                      3   2/Lt. Lovett
                                                      4   War Diary
                                                      5
                                                      6   File.

CAPT.
COMDG. 219 COMPANY M.G. CORPS.

Appendix A.

Transport March Discipline.

1. Turnout.

Special attention will be paid to the turnout of animals, harness and limbers throughout the cove. Animals must be properly groomed and harness and limbers clean whatever the conditions may be.

Special attention will be paid to the packing of limbers, and that limber covers are stretched tight and securely fastened. Head Collar chains must be kept bright and oiled.

2. Halts.

A halt of 10 minutes per hour will be given. Immediately the signal is given, drivers will dismount together, and will loosen girths and look over the animals at once. Drivers will not leave their animals.

All spare horses will be halted with their heads turned towards the centre of the road.

3. Brakesmen.

Brakesmen will march clear of vehicles and no article will be placed on the limber covers. Brakesmen will salute by slinging the rifle and turning head and eyes smartly in the desired direction. THEY WILL NOT SLOPE ARMS.

Only one brakesman per vehicle is to be provided, except the mess cart which may have two.

Brakesmen will march directly behind the limber, and not outside the hub of the wheel.

4. Breakdowns.

If a vehicle breaks down, however short the delay is likely to be, it will be got as far as possible off the road, and the column behind will pass it.

When it has been righted, it will fall into the column wherever it happens to be, and no effort will be made to regain its proper place until a regular halt occurs, and then only if it can be done without blocking the road.

5. Intervals.

Gaps of 25 yards must be left between each section of six vehicles.

[signature] J.F. Allistridt, Capt.
COMDG. 219 COMPANY M.G. CORPS.

Copy No. 1. OC No.1 Section
  "   " 2. OC No 2   "
  "   " 3. OC No 3   "
  "   " 4. OC No 4   "
  "   " 5. HQ.
  "   " 6. WAR DIARY
  "   " 7.
  "   " 8. C.S.M.

219 Machine Gun Company

Appendix No. 5

SECRET

January 25th. 1918

Copy No. 7

Operation Order No. 55

1. Move.

The 219 Machine Gun Company will move from the present area to the ELVERDINGHE area on the afternoon of the 25th.

2. Dress. Full Marching Order. Steel helmets on packs.

3. Limbers.

Limbers to be completely packed by 11.0 a.m. and to be on road facing Camp Entrance by 12.45 p.m. All limbers to be neatly packed and the covers tightly tied down.

Blankets to be put on limbers as far as possible.

4. March Discipline.

Special attention to be paid to march discipline of Transport, especially in regard to mounting and dismounting at halts which will be done by signal from head of column.

5. Rations.

The unconsumed portion of the days rations to be carried on the man.

Dinner 11.30 a.m.
Parade for sections 12.45 p.m.

Issued at 10.10 a.m.
ACKNOWLEDGE.

Copy No. 1   H.Q.
      2   O.C. No. 1 Section
      3   2
      4   3
      5   4
      6   Transport
      7   War Diary.
      8

J. F. Allen, Lieut. CAPT.
COMDG. 219 COMPANY M.G. CORPS.

219 Machine Gun Company   **Appendix No. 6**   SECRET

January 27th. 1918   Copy No. 8

Operation Order No. 56
Map Reference Sheet 28 1/40000
20 S.W.4 1/10000

1. Relief.

No. 3 Section, 219 M.G.Coy, with 8 guns under 2/Lieut. Maxwell, will relieve the 53rd. M.G.Company on the Right Divisional Front, on the morning of January 28th. 1918.

No. 4 Section under 2/Lieut. Lovett will relieve 8 guns of the 216th. M.G.Company on the Left Divisional Front on the morning of January 28th. 1918.

2. Dress.

Fighting Order.

3. Parades.

No. 3 Section will proceed as far as BOESINGHE in two limbers. Seven pack mules will carry rations and equipment---- to parade at 9.0 a.m.

No. 4 Section, personnel, equipment and rations will proceed by train from MANNING CAMP; parade at 9.0 a.m.

4. Guides.

RIGHT SECTOR-- Guides will be at SIGNAL FARM U.21.c.2.0 at 11.0 a.m. to conduct teams to gun positions.

Left Sector--One guides for each gun position will be at LANCIER FARM U.13.d.1.4 at 11.0 a.m.

5. Equipment.

Right Sector--6 tripods, 12 belt boxes per gun and all S.A.A. will be taken over from 53rd. Machine Gun Company.

No. 3 Section will take 8 guns, 2 tripods, 8 spare parts, and all necessary equipment for the line.

Left Sector--16 Belt boxes per gun, A.A. mounting and sights, and S.A.A. will be taken over from 216 M.G.Coy.

No. 4 Section will take 8 guns, 8 tripods, 8 spare parts, and all other necessary equipment for the line.

6. Rations.

Rations for the 28th., 29th., and breakfast rations for the 30th. will be carried.

7. Handing Over.

Receipts will be given for all equipment handed over. All information with reference to lines of fire, dispositions, work in progress and orders will be ascertained before the relieved Companies leave. Care will be taken that all men know the lines of fire of their guns. Receipts for all equipment, and copies of all information will be sent to Company Headquarters immediately.

8. Completion of relief.

Completion of relief will be reported to Company Headquarters by the following code-worDs:-
       Right Sector   STATE
       Left Sector   DURBAR

9. Runners.

Two runners from Company Headquarters, one to each Sector, will accompany Sections, and, having ascertained positions of Line H.Q. will return to Company Headquarters.

Each section will detail one man as runner to be at their headquarters.

10. Command.

TRAINING PROGRAMME.

219 MACHINE GUN COMPANY.

Week ending JANUARY 26th 1918.

DATE	HOUR	NATURE OF TRAINING.	LOCATL.
JAN 21	9 am - 9.45	SQUARE DRILL	
	10 - 11.15	LECTURE "INDIRECT FIRE"	
	11.30 - 12.30.	DEMONSTRATION CANVAS SCREEN	
	2 pm - 2.30.	CLEANING GUNS.	
JAN 22	9 am - 9.45	SQUARE DRILL	
	10 - 11.15	BARRAGE DRILL	
	11.30 - 12.30	STOPPAGES	
	2 pm - 2.30	CLEANING GUNS	
JAN 23	9 am - 9.45	P.T	
	10 - 11.15	LECTURE "CONTOURS IN DEFENCE"	
	11.30 - 12.30	SCHEME "DEFENCE"	
	2 pm - 2.30.	CLEANING GUNS.	
JAN 24	9 am - 9.45	SQUARE DRILL - GAS DRILL	
	10 - 11.15	T.O.E.T. IN BOX RESPIRATORS	
	11.30 - 12.30		
	2 pm - 2.30	CLEANING GUNS.	
JAN 25	9 am - 9.45	SQUARE DRILL	
	10.0 - 11.15	STOPPAGES "Blindfolded"	
	11.30 - 12.30	BARRAGE DRILL	
	2 pm - 2.30	CLEANING GUNS	
JAN 26	9 am - 9.30	SQUARE DRILL	
	10 - 12.30	"DEFENCE OF A VILLAGE"	
	2 pm - 2.30.	CLEANING GUNS.	

10. Command.

Lieut. Elder will establish Advanced Headquarters at CHAMPAUBERT FARM U.14.c.9.4, and will be in charge of both sections.

Issued at 7.0 p.m.

Acknowledge.

Copy No. 1	216 M.G.Coy.
2	53 I.G.Coy.
3	Transport Officer
4	Lieut Elder
5	O.C. No. 3 Section
6	O.C. No. 4 Section
7	Headquarters.
8	
9	War Diary
10	File.

J.F. Allt, Lieutenant,
COMDG. 219 COMPANY M.G. CORPS.

CONFIDENTIAL.

WAR DIARY OF 219TH. MACHINE GUN COMPANY.

From FEBRUARY 1st. 1918   To FEBRUARY 28th. 1918

VOLUME 12.

Army Form C. 2118.

WAR DIARY
or
INTELLIGENCE SUMMARY.
(Erase heading not required.)

Place	Date	Hour	Summary of Events and Information	Remarks and references to Appendices
ELVER-DINGHE AREA	FEB. 1st.		Nos 3 & 4 Sections in the line at U.10.c.00.00. U.9.d.90.00. U.9.c.58.25. U.9.c.30.35. U.8.d.86.54. U.8.d.70.58. U.8.a.55.55. U.7.b.90.55. & U.17.c.60.20. U.17.b.40.20. U.16.c.20.24. U.16.d.10.35. U.15.d.20.70. U.15.d.35.60. U.15.c.alal U.15.c.10.00. Situation Normal.	SHEET A1
do	2		Dispositions Unchanged.	J.F.A.
do	3.		Nos 1 & 2 Sections relieved Nos 3 & 4 Sections in line. Dispositions Unchanged.	J.F.A.
do	4.		Dispositions Unchanged.	J.F.A.
do	5.		Dispositions Unchanged.	J.F.A.
do	6.		Dispositions Unchanged.	J.F.A.
do	7.		Dispositions Unchanged.	J.F.A.
do	8.		Dispositions Unchanged.	J.F.A.
do	9.		Nos 3 & 4 Sections relieved. Nos 1 & 2 Sections in line. Dispositions unchanged.	J.F.A.
do	10.		Company (less Nos 3 & 4 Sections) moved from MANNING CAMP. (B.15.a.3.3.) to BIRKBECK CAMP (A.5.c.20.50). Company settled in billets 2/0 m. Line Dispositions unchanged.	SHEET 28 J.F.A.

WAR DIARY

(Erase heading not required.)

Place	Date	Hour	Summary of Events and Information	Remarks and references to Appendices
WOESTEN AREA	FEB 11		4 Guns at U17c 60.20. U17b 40.20. U16c 20.25. U16.d 10.35. withdrawn from line without Relief. Dispositions of remaining Guns unchanged.	SHEET 21 J.F.A.
do.	12		Company (less Nos 3&4 Sections in line, & Transport [remained at BIRKBECK CAMP.]) moved to NEGRE FM (B34d 90.20) Company settled in Billets at 12.30 p.m. Line dispositions unchanged.	SHEET 28 J.F.A.
BOESINGHE AREA	13.		Dispositions unchanged.	J.F.A.
do	14.		4 Guns at U7b.90.sb. U8a.sr.sr. U8d 70.60. U8d 90.sr. relieved by 97 "Coy M.G.C. Relief complete 3.30 p.m. Dispositions of remaining guns unchanged.	Appendix A. J.F.A.
do	15		Nos 1+2 Sections relieved Nos 3 +4 Sections in line Dispositions unchanged	J.F.A.
do	16		Dispositions unchanged.	J.F.A.
do	17.		Dispositions unchanged.	J.F.A.
do	18.		Company assisted in Operations in Line. Rounds fired 42,000. Operation carried through without mishap.	Appendix 13. J.F.A

Army Form C. 2118.

WAR DIARY

INTELLIGENCE SUMMARY

(Erase heading not required.)

Instructions regarding War Diaries and Intelligence Summaries are contained in F. S. Regs., Part II. and the Staff Manual respectively. Title pages will be prepared in manuscript.

Place	Date	Hour	Summary of Events and Information	Remarks and references to Appendices
BOESINGHE AREA	FEB: 19.		Dispositions Unchanged.	J.F.A.
do.	20.		Dispositions Unchanged.	J.F.A.
do.	21.		Company (less 2 Sections in line, and Transport at BIRKBECK CAMP) moved to BOESINGHE CAMP (35.d.1.7). Company settled in Camp 12 NOON.	SHEET 28
do.	22.		Nos 3&4 Sections relieved Nos 1&2 Sections in Line.	J.F.A.
do.	23.		Dispositions Unchanged.	J.F.A.
do.	24.		Dispositions Unchanged.	J.F.A.
do.	25.		Dispositions Unchanged.	J.F.A.
do.	26.		Relief of 98th M.G. Coy in line. Relief Complete 12 Midnight. Dispositions in line Unchanged.	App:x C. J.F.A.
do.	27.		Transport moved to BLACKMOOR CAMP. Details to BLACKMOOR CAMP. Detail to Steen Camp 11.30 A.M. DEPORT CAMP. Company took part in operations in line. 43,000 Rnds fired All called throuot without mishaps	SHEET 28 App:x D J.F.A.
do.	28.		Dispositions Unchanged. 2.7. Barrage put down with 6 Ing.7a. 20,000 Rounds fired without mishap.	J.F.A. Sheet A1

219 Machine Gun Company

11/2/18

APPENDIX "A"
SECRET

Copy No. 6

Operation Order No. 57

Map Reference BIXSCHOOTE 20 S.W.4 (1/10000)

1. Relief.
Four guns of 219th. Machine Gun Company at U.7.b.90.55, U.8.a.55.55, U.8.a.70.60, U.8.d.90.55, will be relieved by 97th. Machine Gun Company on the morning of February 14th. 1918. Relief to be completed by 3.30 p.m.

2. Guides.
Guides for each gun position will be at Section Headquarters, MONDOVI FARM, U.8.d.55.25 at 10.30 p.m.

3. Equipment.
Four guns, four tripods, spare parts, belt boxes, and all Company property to be taken out of vacated positions, and disposed as directed by Lieut. Elder until 15/2/18.

4. Handing Over.
Receipts will be prepared in duplicate for all stores handed over, one copy being sent to Company Headquarters after relief. All information regarding lines of fire, work in progress, will be handed over to 97th. M.G.Company.

5. Completion of Relief.
Completion of Relief to be reported to Company Headquarters by Code word "EXPRESS"

After relief the teams will be attached to remaining guns in the line as directed by 2/Lieut. Lord.

ACKNOWLEDGE.
Issued at 2.30 p.m.

Copy No. 1 H.Q.
2. 97 M.G.Coy.
3. 2/Lt. Lord
4. Lt. Elder
5. War Diary
6.
7. File.

J.F. Allan Licht
CAPT.
COMDG. 219 COMPANY M.G. CORPS.

219 Machine Gun Company APPENDIX "B"
                        SECRET

February 18th. 1918   Copy No. 6

Operation Order No. 58

Map Reference Sheet A.1   1/10000

1. **Information.**

   On Monday night 18/19th. inst. the 96th. and 97th. Infantry
   Brigades will carry out raids on enemy positions as under at
   an hour to be notified later.

   96th. Inf.Brigade.   Dugouts and pillboxes, etc. along road from
                          U.4.c.9.4 to cross-roads at U.5.a.9.9
                          inclusive including HOWARD FARM.

   97th. Inf.Brigade.   (a) On area in vicinity of BORCOUFF FARM
                              U.4.a.85.25
                          (b) On area just South of M in ZEVECOTEN
                              about U.3.b.85.35

2. **Objects.**

   (a) To kill or capture any enemy found in above areas.
   (b) To obtain identifications.
   (c) To secure M.Gs, T.Ms or other booty.

3. **Artillery.**

   (a) The Divisional Artillery will bring an intense bombardment
       to bear on places to be raided from Zero to Zero plus 8
       minutes.
   (b) At Zero plus 8 minutes artillery will lift on to selected
       points and barrage line in rear and infantry will rush and
       capture posts.
   (c) At Zero plus 20 minutes fire of artillery will slacken,
       ceasing altogether at Zero plus 30 minutes.

4. **Machine Guns.**

   All available machine guns in line, with 8 additional guns, will
   assist in above operations.
                219
5. **Action of Machine Gun Company.**

   Two 4-gun Batteries of 219 M.G.Company at U.9.c.25.37 and U.9.a.
   90.85 will put down a standing barrage at Zero on a line running
   from U.33.a.90.80 to U.34.a.05.20.
   Fire to be maintained at 120 rds. per min. until Zero plus 30
   From Zero plus 30 the guns will stand by ready to open fire at
   once on to same line in reply to S.O.S. or special orders.
   Detailed firing instructions issued separately to Battery
   Commanders.
   The four guns at CRADDLE FARM, U.15 central and U.15.a.8.70 will
   move into position at U.9.a.90.85 on afternoon of 18th.
   The four guns at present at RHONE FARM will move into position
   at U.9.c.25.37 on afternoon of 18th.
   All guns to be in position ready to fire by Zero minus 60 minutes
   Ammunition for all guns will be made up to to 20 beltboxes per
   gun and 4 boxes S.A.A.
   "T" bases and "T" aiming marks will be employed.
   Every care will be taken to prevent short shooting.
   A fire base and depression stops are essential.
   Sandbag screens will be provided to conceal flash.
   At Zero plus 60 minutes, the 4 guns from CRADDLE FARM will
   return to the position and lay on set lines of fire.
   The 4 guns from RHONE FARM will be withdrawn and return to camp.

6. **Synchronisation of Watches**

   Watches will be synchronised from Company Headquarters at CRADDLE

FARM at 4 p.m.

O.20.--DIRECTIVES:

A post on the line laid at U.9.c.25.27 will be manned by Company Signallers and communication will be kept up from there with CRAONNE FARM.

Issued at 12 noon.

ACKNOWLEDGE.

J. Faulkner .... CAPT.
COMDG. 219 COMPANY M.G. CORPS.

Copy No. 1   H.Q.
        2   D.Hdq.Co
        3   Lt. Elder
        4   2/Lt. Betts
        5
        6   War Diary
        7   File.

219 Machine Gun Company

APPENDIX "C"
SECRET

February 25th. 1918

Copy No. 2

Operation Order No. 59

1. **Relief.**

    Seven guns of 96th. M.G.Company will be relieved by 219th. M.G. Company on the Right Divisional Front at FAIDHERBE CROSS ROADS (2 guns), UCKAELD (2 guns), LONELY MILL (2 Guns) and U.10.d.1.1 (1 gun)

    Two guns at U.9.d.90.00 and four guns at CRAONNE FARM at present manned by 219th. M.G.Coy. will be relieved by 96th. M.G.Coy.

2. **Guides.**

    Guides for each position from 96th. Company will be at LANCIER CROSS ROADS at 5.0 p.m., except those for U.10.d.1.1, which will be at SIGNAL FARM.

    Guides for positions at present manned by 219 Company will be at CRAONNE FARM at 5.0 p.m.

3. **Equipment.**

    219 Company will take in 7 guns, spare parts, condensor bags and tubes. 6 guns and spare parts will be taken out by relieved teams.

4. **Handing Over.**

    All remaining stores will be handed over.
    Receipts will be prepared in duplicate for all stores handed over, one copy being sent to Company Headquarters after relief. All information regarding lines of fire, work in progress will be handed over by relieved teams in all cases.

5. **Completion of Relief.**

    Completion of relief to be reported to Company Headquarters at CRAONNE FARM, by code word "EAGLE"

6. **Command.**

    After reliefs, the guns of 96th. Company and 219th. Company will be under the command of O.C. 219th. M.G.Company with Headquarters at CRAONNE FARM, where all reports as to situation, work done, casualties and rounds fired will be sent by 6.0 a.m. daily.

Issued at 4.0 p.m.

Acknowledge.

..................................CAPT.
COMDG. 219 COMPANY M.G. CORPS.

Copy No. 1 H.Q.
2 96 M.G.Coy.
3. 2/Lt. Morley
4. 2/Lt. Maxwell
5
6 War Diary
7 File.

219th. Machine Gun Company

APPENDIX "D"
SECRET

February 27th. 1918

Copy No. 5

Operation Order No. 60

Map Reference:- Sheet A.1   1/10000

1. Information.

(a) On night of 29th. inst. the 14th. and 96th. Infantry Brigades will carry out raids on the enemy positions, at an hour to be announced later.
  (a) 14th. Brigade Area in U.4.a.4.6 and O.34.d.
  (b) 96th. Brigade MARACHAL FARM O.36.d.1.1.

2. Objects.
  1. To kill or capture any Germans found in the area.
  2. To obtain identifications, and documents.

3. Artillery.
  (a) The Field Artillery will provide standing protective barrages around the Area to be attacked.
  (b) It will also provide a creeping barrage under which the Infantry will advance.
  (c) Howitzers and H.A. will concentrate on special areas and avenues of approach., to isolate the parts to be attacked as much as possible.

4. Machine Guns.

Vickers' guns will co-operate in both raids.

5. Action of 219 M.G.Coy.

A battery of 9 guns at U.11.a.1.0 will put down a barrage on line running from P.31.c.15.85 to V.1.a.36.80
Fire to be opened at Zero plus 12 and maintained at 60 rds. per minute until Zero plus 80.
After which guns will stand by ready to open fire immediately at Zero plus 3 hours 15 minutes , (Rate 60 rds. per min. each gun to fire four belts.) until Zero plus 3 hours 30 mins.
Detailed firing instructions issued separately to Battery Commanders and Officers concerned.
The 2 guns at U.9.c.25.37 will move into positions at U.11.a.1.0 on afternoon of "Z" day.
The 2 guns at LONELY MILL and 3 gun at U.10.d.1.1 will move into position at U.11.a.1.0 on afternoon of "Z" day.
Guns from DEKORT CAMP will move up at same time.
All guns to be in prsition ready to fire by Zero minus 30 mins.
Ammunition for all guns to be made up into 20 boxes per gun.
Also 2 cans water per gun, "T" Bases and "T" aiming marks being employed.
Screens will be used to conceal the flash, but the aiming mark must be kept visible.
Every care must be taken to prevent short shooting; a firm base and depression stops are essential.
Allowance to be made for error of day will be issued later.
A report that all guns are in position will be sent in at Zero minus 30 minutes.
Further reports at Zero plus 30, 60 and 90 mins. will be sent in to Company Headquarters.
At Zero plus 3 hours 30 minutes, guns will resume their normal positions in line, guns from DEKORT CAMP returning there.

6. Synchronisation of watches.

Time will be issued later by Battalion Headquarters.

7. Communications.

219th. Company will run a line from Company Hd.Qrs.(CRAONNE) to

to
    to battery p at U.11.a.1.0

    96 Company will lay a line from there to LOUVOIS Farm.

8. Action of 96th. M.G.Company

    96th. Company will put down a barrage on a line from O.36.b.40.15 to P.31.c.15.85 from Battery position at LOUVOIS FARM.

    Fire to be opened at Zero plus 12 mins. and maintained at 60 rds per min. until Zero plus 80.

    The guns will then stand by until Zero plus 3 hours 15 mins., when fire will be re-opened at a rate of 60 rds. per min.
(4 beltboxes per gun to be fired)

    Guns to be in position at Zero minus 30 mins.
The general directions for 219th. Company will apply to few of 96th Company.

    All guns to return to their normal line positions at Zero plus 3 hours 30 minutes.

9. Refilling belts.

    Arrangements will be made for refilling belts as soon as emptied.

Issued at 11.0 a.m.

ACKNOWLEDGE.

                                        Copy No. 1 H.Q.
                                                      2. D.M.G.C.
                                                      3. 96th.M.G.Coy.
                                                      4. Lt. Elder
                                                      5. Lt. Smith
                                                      6.
                                                      7. War Diary
                                                      8. File.

                            for Lieut.
            Cmdg. Right Divl. Machine Guns.

www.ingramcontent.com/pod-product-compliance
Lightning Source LLC
Chambersburg PA
CBHW081409160426
43193CB00013B/2140